INTERNATIONALES JAHRBUCH
KOMMUNIKATIONSDESIGN

INTERNATIONAL YEARBOOK
COMMUNICATION DESIGN

1999/2000

HERAUSGEGEBEN VON / EDITED BY PETER ZEC

Internationales Jahrbuch Kommunikationsdesign
International Yearbook Communication Design
1999/2000

Herausgegeben von / Edited by Peter Zec

avedition

IMPRESSUM
IMPRINT

Herausgeber/Editor	Peter Zec
Übersetzung/Translation	Vineeta Manglani
Redaktion/Editorial	Petra Kiedaisch, Eva Wittwer
Gestaltung/Design	Julia Kleiner, **av**communication GmbH
Produktion/Production	Gunther Heeb, **av**communication GmbH
Litho/Lithographie	Corinna Rieber, **av**communication GmbH
Druck/Printing	Leibfarth + Schwarz GmbH + Co. KG, Dettingen/Erms
Papier/Paper	150 g/m² Dullcoat

Der Deutsche Preis für Kommunikationsdesign wird von der Stadt Essen und der Messe Essen gefördert.

The German Prize for Communication Design is promoted by the town of Essen and the Trade Fair Centre in Essen.

©Copyright 2000 **av**edition GmbH, Ludwigsburg

Alle Rechte vorbehalten
All Rights reserved

ISBN 3-929638-33-9
Printed in Germany

INHALT
CONTENTS

Vorwort des Herausgebers	6
Peter Zec	
Welch kein Wunder	10
Kurt Weidemann	
Grand Prix	18
Die prämierten Arbeiten	
Juniorpreis	22
Höchste Designqualität	26
Werbung	56
Unternehmenskommunikation	80
Produktkommunikation	120
Fernsehen und elektronische Medien	124
Kultur und Sport	130
Verlagswesen	148
Multimedia	170
Die Form der Kommunikation?	192
Peter Zec	
Anhang	196

Preface by the Editor	7
Peter Zec	
What a Surprise	14
Kurt Weidemann	
Grand Prix	18
The Prize Winners	
Junior Prize	22
Highest Design Quality	26
Advertising	56
Corporate Communications	80
Product Communications	120
Television and Electronic Media	124
Culture and Sport	130
Publishing	148
Multimedia	170
The Form of Communication?	194
Peter Zec	
Appendix	196

Vorwort des Herausgebers

Preface by the editor

»Die zehn Gebote enthalten 279 Wörter, die amerikanische Unabhängigkeitserklärung 300 Wörter, die Verordnung der Europäischen Gemeinschaft über den Import von Karamelbonbons aber exact 25.911 Wörter.« (Zitat, Quelle unbekannt)

Wer immer sich einmal die Mühe des Zählens gemacht hat, hat verstanden: Kommunikation ist zwar alles, aber auch ihre Vermittlung muß stimmen. Wenn ein Inhalt und dessen Darstellung in einer falschen Relation zueinander stehen, wird Kommunikation zumindest erschwert, wenn nicht gar unmöglich. »Gutes Kommunikationsdesign muß im wahrsten Sinne des Wortes kommunizieren, einen Lebensstil zum Ausdruck bringen und Werte vermitteln. Es muß eine Verführung zur Information stattfinden, ein intuitives und gefühlsmäßiges Aufnehmen von den vermittelten Inhalten. Gutes Kommunikationsdesign spricht zuerst den Bauch an und setzt sich dann im Kopf fest«, so Hans Brandt, Mitglied der diesjährigen Jury für den Deutschen Preis für Kommunikationsdesign.

Um die »gute Form«, die im Industriedesign eine so große Rolle spielt, auch in der Kommunikation zu fördern, schreibt das Design Zentrum Nordrhein Westfalen seit 1993 den Deutschen Preis für Kommunikationsdesign aus. Der Erfolg zeigt uns, daß es in der Tat ein steigendes Bedürfnis nach Qualifizierung in diesem Bereich gibt. Jedes Jahr nimmt die Zahl der Bewerbungen um den Preis zu. In diesem Jahr nahmen 894 Designer und 100 Auftraggeber aus 11 Ländern mit insgesamt 2.327 Arbeiten am Wettbewerb teil. Dabei wurden 27 Auszeichnungen für »Höchste« und 120 für »Hohe« Designqualität vergeben.

Die bisher sehr hohe Qualität der Einsendungen wurde auch bei dieser Ausschreibung gehalten, wenn auch anders als in den letzten Jahren: Waren die Jurierungen bislang oft von polarisierenden Diskussionen geprägt, da die Arbeiten qualitativ alle auf einem ähnlichen Level waren, hatte es die Jury in diesem Jahr leichter, denn die Einsendungen variierten deutlicher als bisher. Deshalb fiel es der Jury auch nicht schwer, die herausragenden Arbeiten des Jahres mit dem Grand Prix und dem in diesem Jahr erstmals ausgeschriebenen Juniorpreis zu bedenken: Der Grand Prix ging an die niederländische Agentur Limage dangereuse, der Juniorpreis an die in Essen ansässige Jung-Designerin Tamara Narolski für ihr bemerkenswertes Werk »Wenn die Nacht kein Ende nimmt«.

Die Ergebnisse dieses Wettbewerbs werden wie in jedem Jahr im vorliegenden Buch dokumentiert. Es versteht sich jedoch nicht nur als reiner Katalog, sondern als Nachschlagewerk für den täglichen Gebrauch. Immer wieder erfahren wir, daß Designer, Agenturen und Unternehmen sich wertvolle Anregungen aus dem Buch holen. Aber auch für Personalberater hat es sich als Servicehandbuch bei der Suche nach neuen Talenten bewährt. Deshalb freue ich mich, Ihnen wieder ein spannendes Buch zum Schmökern und Stöbern an die Hand geben zu können.

Auch in diesem Jahr möchte ich natürlich an dieser Stelle denen danken, die die Durchführung des Wettbewerbs mit möglich gemacht haben, im besonderen der Messe Essen, die das Preisgeld von DM 20.000,-- für den Grand Prix bereitgestellt hat, aber auch der Stadt Essen sowie den beteiligten Designverbänden AGD (Allianz Deutscher Designer), BDG (Bund Deutscher Grafik-Designer), BFF (Bund Freischaffender Foto-Designer) und VGD (Verband der Grafik-Designer). Nicht zuletzt gilt unser Dank natürlich den Juroren und allen Teilnehmern, die mit ihren teils sehr mutigen und kreativen Einsendungen auch diesen Wettbewerb wieder zu einem Erlebnis gemacht haben.

Ihr Prof. Dr. Peter Zec

»The ten commandments consist of 279 words, the American Declaration of Independence 300 words, but the European Community regulation on the importing of caramel sweets has exactly 25, 911 words.« (Quote, Source unknown)

Anyone who has ever bothered with counting will have understood: communication is everything - but its transference has to be correct as well. If content and the representation thereof stand in the wrong relation to one another, communication will at least be made more difficult, if not impossible. »Good communication design has, in the truest sense of the word, to communicate, express a lifestyle and transport values. The information has to seduce and an intuitive and instinctive reception of the contents has to be transmitted. Good communication design initially appeals to the gut and then establishes itself in the intellect«, says Hans Brandt, member of this year's jury for the German Prize for Communication Design.

In order to also encourage the »good form«, which plays such a large role in industrial design, in communication, the Design Zentrum Nordrhein Westfalen has been offering the German Prize for Communication Design since 1993. The success shows us that there actually is an increasing need for qualification in this area. The number of entries for the prize increases each year. This year 894 designers and 100 clients from 11 countries took part in the competition, submitting a total of 2,327 works. Amongst these, 27 awards were presented for the »highest« design quality and 120 for »high« design quality.

The high standard of entries submitted up tell now was also maintained, although the entries differed from previous years. If the juries up to now had been characterised by polarising discussions, since the works were qualitatively on a similar level, then the jury had it easier this year as the entries varied more significantly than before. Therefore the jury did not find it difficult to award the Grand Prix as well as the Junior Prize, awarded for the first time this year, to the excellent works submitted this year. The Grand Prix went to the Dutch agency Limage dangereuse; the Junior Prize went to Tamara Narolski, a young designer based in Essen, for her remarkable work entitled »When the night never ends«.

The results of the competition have been documented in this book, as every year. But it should not purely be considered as a catalogue. It should be seen as a reference work for daily use.

We are increasingly discovering that designers, agencies and companies get worthwhile stimulus from the book. But the book has also proved itself in aiding Personnel consultants in their search for new talent. This is why I am pleased to be able to present you with an exciting book to browse and comb through.

Of course, I would also like to take the opportunity this year of thanking those who helped to make the realisation of this competition possible.

I would particularly like to thank the Trade Fair Centre in Essen which provided the 20,000 DM prize money for the Grand Prix, and also the city of Essen as well as the design associations involved - AGD (Allianz Deutscher Designer), BDG (Bund Deutscher Grafik-Designer), BFF (Bund Freischaffender Foto-Designer) and VGD (Verband der Grafik-Designer). And last but not least, we would like to thank the jurors and all participants who sent in their creative, and sometimes very courageous, entries. They have once again turned this competition into an experience.

Yours Prof. Dr. Peter Zec

Welch kein Wunder

Kurt Weidemann

Das Jahrhundert neigt sich in Nachdenklichkeit. Die Verehrung der Deutschen für das Dezimalsystem beginnt schon bei »runden Geburtstagen« (da ist immer eine Null dabei). Jahrhundertwenden werden schon mit Orakeln und Menetekeln bedacht. Eine Jahrtausendwende, drei Nullen, erlebt – nach heutigem Stand der Lebenserwartung – nur jede dreiundreißigste Generation.

Unser Denken erfaßt und begreift noch einen Zeitraum unterhalb eines Jahrhunderts, der uns als Lebensglück oder Daseinslast beschert oder auferlegt wurde. Zeit steht nicht still. Da es ein Jahr null nicht gegeben hat, feiern wir die drei Nullen ein Jahr zu früh. Welch kein Wunder. Zeit – davon haben wir alle gleich viel – ist deshalb auch die gerechteste Sache der Welt. Zukunft kann man nicht im Rückspiegel sehen, wer aber nicht weiß, was hinter ihm liegt, hat es schwerer, zu erkennen, was vor ihm ist und sein wird.

In den Berufen, die sich um die angewandte Kunst und um die Kommunikation angesiedelt haben, scheint die Uhr schneller zu laufen, die Aktualität kurzfristiger zu sein, der Erfolg flüchtiger zu verweilen, die Berufsfähigkeit schneller zu verblassen. Wer das wenige Jahrzehnte überlebt hat, wird bereits als Designosaurier von der nächsten Generation ignoriert.

In der Ratlosigkeit der Gegenwart wird der Abschied von ihr durch verlorengegangene Lebenssinnbewältigung offenbart: Im Freizeitverhalten wird beim Himalaja-Trekking, beim Freeclimbing, Canyoning und Haifischtauchen die lust- und gefahrenvolle Vermählung mit den Elementen gesucht und das Umkommen riskiert. Die Ausstattung dafür entwerfen Designer: Für die Produktion von Gebrauchsgütern drängt man sie mehr und mehr in die Abschiebehaft: Wie ärmlich, bedrückend und trübsinnig muß das Leben derer sein, die den Kick des Abenteuerurlaubes brauchen. Selbst eine Ehe kann langanhaltend abenteuerlicher sein.

Deshalb ist Competition angesagt. Competition belebt das Geschäft, die muß natürlich world wide oder global sein. Manche Wettbewerbe übertreffen in ihrer Häufigkeit die Zahl auszeichnungswürdiger Einrichtungen, andere sind so reich beschickt, daß Preiswürdiges unberücksichtigt bleiben muß. Risiken sind nicht auszuschließen. Irrtum ist vorbehaltlich.

Das Jahrtausend entläßt uns in keinen Zustand hoffnungsvoller Freude. Wahllos kann man dafür ein paar Ängste herausgreifen:
- Das nach wie vor grandiose Potential atomarer Waffen und die unbeherrschte Atomenergie können diesem Erdball hundertfach den Garaus machen.
- Der Raubbau an den Reserven der Natur, die zunehmend wütender mit ihren Elementen zurückschlägt.
- Der Eingriff des Menschen in Bereiche, die bisher der Schöpfungsgeschichte vorbehalten waren: gentechnisch manipulierte und geklonte Retortenwesen und Produkte – (Ein Designerauftrag?)
- Wachsende Störungen und Schäden in den Beziehungen zwischen Körper – Geist – Seele. Menschenrechtsappelle werden mit brutalen Verletzungen beantwortet.

»Kalt und unpersönlich« nennt Steven Weinberg den Gegenwartsmenschen. Wo trifft man noch in den flotten Modeberufen (unsere einschließlich) einen königlichen Kaufmann? Oder Menschen hoher Bildung und persönlicher Kultur? Unzeitgemäße Begriffe wie Gesinnungsethik oder Verantwortungsethik werden, als nicht ganz von dieser Welt, bei den Wolkenträumern belächelt. Wer gebend und helfend uneigennützig handelt, wird allerdings gern beansprucht und dann stillschweigend unter die nützlichen Idioten eingeordnet. Welch kein Wunder.

Die Sprünge und Prognosen, die das elektronische Zeitalter einläuten, von den einen als Friedensgeläut, von den anderen als Feuerglocken verstanden, treffen die Design-Berufe unschlüssig, beharrend, zwiespältig. Das Tagesgeschäft wird zügig und auf gutem bis beachtlichem Niveau bewältigt. Ein geistiger Aufbruch ist nicht zu spüren, von der Designer-Szene auch nicht gerade zu erwarten. Wenn es um den Erklärungsbedarf dieser Welt geht, werden die Astrophysiker die Philosophen des kommenden Jahrhunderts sein. Ein Schluck aus dem Weihwasserbecken der reinen Erkenntnis soll sie auf der Suche nach der »Weltformel« stärken.

Erstaunlicherweise sind sie sich einig, daß diese Formel »unausweichlich schön« sein muß (Steven Weinberg). Die Formel soll zu einem tieferen Verständnis, die Begriffe Eleganz, Einfachheit, Schönheit und Wahrheit zueinander führen, nicht anders zu ersetzen und nicht mehr zu verbessern sein. Das hört sich an wie ein Universalbekenntnis der Design-Berufe: elegant, einfach, schön und wahr, nicht mehr zu verbessern.

Die emotionalen Faktoren im grand Design werden von präzisen Denkstrukturen durchsetzt, die den genialen Künstlerentwurf aussparen, ignorieren. Neid, Ehrgeiz und Eitelkeit finden dann keine so üppige Nahrung mehr. Sollte Schönheit als Beweis der Wahrheit herauskommen, werden wir gut zu tun bekommen. Die Jubelfürsprecher virtueller Welten, die im Tempo der elektronischen Generationswechsel zu Millionären und Milliardären geworden sind, was ihnen gegönnt sei, haben keine Zeit, Schatten zu beleuchten und Folgen abzuschätzen.

Die Halbwertzeit des Wissens in der Computerbranche ist auf wenige Jahre geschrumpft. Ein »Internetjahr« wird mit drei Monaten angegeben. Ein Jahreseinkommen kann man dabei in der gleichen Zeit verdienen. Die Produktionsausstattung des Modells Mensch hat in ihrer Entwicklungsgeschichte viele Anpassungsentwürfe erfahren, dennoch schleppt er immer noch eine Menge Adam/Eva mit sich herum. Im Monopoly der Computergenerationen wird das ohne flammende Begeisterung, vielmehr mit cooler Nüchternheit durchgespielt.

Fragen sind Experimente. Der Computer als Abwandlungsspielzeug im Design angewendet, hilft gar nichts, wenn man weder Geschmack noch Urteilskraft hat, noch weiß, was man eigentlich will. Arbeitsteilung ist dabei so primitiv wie Zellteilung bei Kleinlebewesen oder wie die Schaffung neuer Beamtenstellen zur Problemerweiterung.

Nachdenklich macht, wenn Wissenschaftler und Erfinder der ersten Computergeneration längst begonnen haben, die Computer-Mythen zu entlarven, das Internet als reichste Quelle des Nonsens zu bezeichnen und ihre Erkenntnisse wie der berühmte Computerwissenschaftler Joseph Weizenbaum in einem kurzen Satz zusammenzufassen: »Wunderschön, alles Quatsch!«. Das Internet hat derweil seine Nützlichkeit lawinenartig fest begründet und wird zweifelsfrei seinen Lawinengang mit Donnergetöse fortsetzen. Niemand durchschaut dieses Betriebssystem, erkennt, daß es anders reagiert als beabsichtigt. Außer daß es bequemer ist, im Netz einzukaufen als mit dem Einkaufsnetz über die Straße zu gehen, werden wir uns auch daran gewöhnen, daß es eine elektronische Intelligenz geben wird, die schneller, umfangreicher und fehlerfreier arbeitet als unsere eigene.

Nebenbei wird durch die absoluten virtuellen Freiheiten das Urheberrecht an Bild, Ton und Gestalt vor die Hunde gehen. Die Vielfalt der Manipulationen und Unzahl der Zugriffe jederzeit an jedem Ort wird eine wirksame Kontrolle der Aneignungen und Kopien unmöglich machen.

Konjunktur haben heute – auch wieder in unseren Berufsgruppen:
- Design-Friseure, die versuchen, auf einer Glatze eine Locke zu drehen: als crossculture-Spezialisten.
- Trickkünstler, die minderen Produkten mit Neppdesign und Mogelpackungen Attraktivität andienen
- Verkaufskanonen, die gerupften Hühnern die Füße breitklopfen, um sie als Enten loszuschlagen.

In einem Land, in dem die Mentalität, Kinder und Hunde an der Leine zu führen, das Rasen betreten zu verbieten immer noch ihre Parteigänger hat, ist der Ruf nach Innovationsschüben und Querdenkern, eine glatte Hohldonnerei.

Die Intension, die Eingebung ist der Gestaltungsfaktor, nicht der Computer als Variantenschleuder und Zufallsgenerator. Gestaltung setzt unvoreingenommene, intensive Anschauung voraus. Intensive Anschauung erfolgt konzentriert, zielstrebig, ausdauernd, fleißig und sorgfältig und bildet die Urteilsfähigkeit. Risikofreudigkeit und der Mut, seine Fähigkeiten selbst richtig einzuschätzen, wird Entscheidungen mit einer selbstverständlichen Richtigkeit herbeiführen. In den vorgeburtlichen neun Monaten fällt man seine Entscheidungen noch zwangsläufig aus dem Bauch. Manche halten sich ein Leben lang daran.

Die Design-Szene ist »wertepluralistisch«, das ist ein besseres Wort für ratlos. Form follows – immer noch function. Und in den meisten Fällen ist das auch vernünftig. Auch wenn sich die Funktionen bis zur Unsichtbarkeit auf den Chip verkrümelt haben. Auge, Hand, Erkennen, Verstehen, Begreifen halten mit den Innovationsschüben und Generationswechseln der Geräte im Babyalter längst nicht mehr Schritt. Form follows fun oder fiction oder fantasy: Dafür haben wir alle ein zu gemäßigtes Klima.

Ausgerechnet dort, wo es am wenigsten zu innovieren gibt, werden die durchgeknalltesten Befreiungsschläge gemacht: in der Typographie. Was kein Wunder. Dort gibt es leider die an unseren Augen, unseren Lebensgewohnheiten und der Form der Buchstaben erprobten Regeln, die sich seit Gutenberg nicht verändert, also bewährt, haben. Eher sind wir oberflächlicher, ungeduldiger, gehetzter geworden. Nur die Textherstellung hat sich hochbeschleunigt, aber unsere Fähigkeit zu sehen und zu verstehen nicht. Die Adepten auf den Spuren von Neville Brody, David Carson, Tibor Kalman folgen ihnen ungelenk und zaghaft: ein schaler, zweiter Aufguß. Wir können sowas nicht besonders gut.

Als der C_W-Wert im Automobildesign der Verringerung des Luftwiderstandes zuliebe rundgelutschte Gummibärchen vorschrieb und alles gleich langweilig aussah, zeigte der Rolls-Royce unbeeindruckt weiter seine kantigen Bügelfalten. Das Cockpit wurde in einer brillanten Besprechung mit »wirr, planlos und schön« charakterisiert. Diesem Designmanko sind keine Unfallserien und Rückrufaktionen ins Werk gefolgt (der Besitzer saß auch selten selbst am Volant).

Wir werden unter sehr anderen Umständen weiterleben: Das Weiche, Nebelhafte, Abstrakte drängt sich immer mehr und tiefer in das Konkrete, Dinghafte, Sichtbare. Das unseren Fingern, mit denen wir bisher unsere Arbeit gemacht haben, nicht mehr Be-greif-liche auf Bildschirmen, in Datenspeichern, Filmen, Programmen, nimmt überhand. Die Gesellschaft unserer Breitengrade wird nicht mehr überwiegend mit dem Entwerfen und Herstellen von Produkten befaßt sein, mit ihrem Verkaufen, Verbrauchen oder Sammeln, sondern sich mit dem Gewinn von Erlebnissen, Erfahrungen, Kenntnissen, dem Vermitteln von Informationen zuwenden.

Auf der Suche nach einer »Theorie für Alles und Jedes« ist es einmal wieder mehr der Glaube, als das Wissen, der zum Enträtseln der Fragen nach eleganten Formeln für den Weltenlauf führt. Welche Lawinen sich durch das immerwährende globale Einspeisen dort zusammenklumpen, wann sie, wo und wohin mit welchen Folgen abgehen, das ist, nach Art der Lawinen, nicht genau zu berechnen.

Für die Designberufe wird es eine Abwendung von bildender künstlerischer Potenz in Richtung intelligenter Übereinkunft und Manipulation freier gesellschaftlicher Bedürfnisse geben. Die Hände müssen nichts mehr behandeln, sondern nur berühren und tasten. Die Miniaturgerätschaften werden durch Sprache gesteuert. Das Geistige in der Kunst wird nicht mehr mit der Hand gemacht.

Wir führen immer perfekter und raffinierter ein Leben zweiter und dritter Hand. Fernsehen, Internet, elektronische Unterhaltungsmedien degenerieren das überanstrengte Gehör und Auge. Nur wenn man sich noch direkt, unverstellt und offen begegnet, kann man seinen Augen noch trauen.

Ich habe fertig.
Was kein Wunder. Sag ich mal so.
Das Wetter

What a Surprise

Kurt Weidemann

The century weighs heavy with a pensiveness. The German admiration for the decimal system begins with »round« birthdays (always with a nought in them). Turns of the century are already presented with oracles and omens. A millennium is only experienced by every 33rd generation – according to current life expectancy.

Our thinking still comprehends a period of time within a century which was either bestowed on us as a piece of luck or inflicted on us as an existential burden. Time does not stand still. As there was no year zero, we are celebrating the three zeros a year too early. What a surprise. Time, since everyone has an equal amount of it, is thus the fairest thing in the world. The future cannot be seen in the rear view mirror, but if we don't know what is behind us, it is more difficult to recognise what lies in front of us and what will happen in the future.

In those professions which have established themselves around the applied arts and communication, it seems as if time passes by more swiftly, current events are more short-lived, success is more fleeting and professional competence pales quicker. Whoever has survived the fewest decades is ignored as a designosaur by the next generation.

In the helplessness of the present taking one's leave of it is revealed though lost attempts at coping with the meaning of life. In leisure activities such as trekking in the Himalayas, free-climbing, canyoning and shark diving, a pleasurable and dangerous marriage with the elements is pursued by putting one's life at risk. The ideas for equipment for these activities are dreamt up by designers. In the production of consumer durables they are increasingly pushed towards a situation verging on deportation: how tragic, depressing and dull a person's life must be if they need the kick of an adventure holiday. Even a marriage can be more adventurous in the long-term.

Competition is thus necessary. Competition injects life into business and must, of course, be world-wide or global. The frequency of some competitions exeeds the number of entries worthy of an award; others receive so many entries that often those deserving an award have to be disregarded. Risks are not to be ruled out. The right to err is reserved.

The century is not retiring under hopeful circumstances. We can pick out a few of our fears at random:

- The fantastic potential of atomic weapons and uncontrolled atomic energy, which is still capable of destroying the earth a hundred times over.
- The overexploitation of reserves of nature, whose elements are striking back with an ever-increasing fury.
- People's interference in areas which had previously been left to the Story of Creation: genetically manipulated and cloned test-tube beings and products (the commissioned job of a designer?).
- Growing disturbances in, and damage to, the relationship between body – spirit – soul. Appeals for human rights are answered with brutal injuries.

Steven Weinberg calls present day people »cold and impersonal«. Where can we still meet a regal businessperson in the racy, fashionable professions (including ours)? Or highly-educated or cultured people? Outmoded terms such as »ethical behaviour« or »ethical responsibility«, not really being of this world, are readily adopted of them. In the end they are quietly categorised as useful idiots. What a surprise.

The design occupations meet with indecisiveness, insistence and conflicting feelings, the leaps and prognoses that are ringing in the electronic age, seen by some as bells ringing in peace and by others as a fire alarm.

Daily business is still dealt with briskly, the standard being good to remarkable. There are no signs of an intellectual departure and neither is this to be expected from the design scene. When it comes to the need to explain the world, the astrophysicists will be the philosophers of the next century. A sip from the holy water font of pure knowledge should give them strength in their search for a »world formula«.

Astonishingly, they are in agreement that the formula has to be »unavoidably beautiful« (Steven Weinberg). This formula should lead to a deeper understanding, to a connection between the terms elegance, simplicity, beauty and truth and should be both irreplaceable and perfect. This sounds like a universal confession of the design professions: elegant, simple, beautiful and real, which cannot be improved.

The emotional factors in grand design are achieved by precise thought structures which omit and ignore an artist's brilliant design. Envy, ambition and vanity then no longer find such opulent nourishment. If Beauty should emerge as the proof of Truth, we would have our work cut out for us. The enthusiastic advocates of virtual worlds, who have become millionaires and billionaires at the speed of the electronic alternation of generations – which we do not begrudge them - do not have the time to illuminate shadows and estimate consequences.

The half-life of knowledge in the computer business has shrunk to a few years. An »internet year« is given as 3 months. An annual income can be earned in the same amount of time. The product equipment for the Human Being Model has experienced a lot of adaptations in design in the history of evolution, however it still drags a lot of Adam/Eve about with it. In the monopoly of the computer generations this is acted through with cool sobriety, not heated enthusiasm.

Questions are experiments. The computer is used as a modifying toy in design. But this does not help if we have neither taste nor the power to judge and do not know what we really want. The division of work is as is primitive here as cell division with micro-organisms or the creation of new jobs in the civil service to extend the problem.

What is thought-provoking is when scientists and inventors of the first computer generation began long ago to expose computer myths, label the internet as the richest source of nonsense and summarise their knowledge in a short sentence »Great, it's all rubbish!«, as did the computer scientist Joseph Weizenbaum.

In the meantime the internet has solidly justified its usefulness, in an avalanche-like fashion, and will, no doubt, continue along its avalanche course with a thundering crash. No-one sees through this operating system and recognises that it reacts other than intended.

Apart from the fact that it is more comfortable to go shopping on the Net than across the street with a basket, we will also become used to the fact that an electronic intelligence will exist which will work faster and more extensively and faultlessly than our own.

At the same time, due to this absolute virtual freedom, the copyright of images, sound and design will go to the dogs. The great number of manipulative variations and countless possibilities of access at any place, any time, render the effective monitoring of the acquisitions and copies impossible.

The following are experiencing an economic boom – again in our professional groups:
- Designer hairdressers who attempt to create a curl on a bald head: as cross-culture specialists.
- Con artists who attempt to make inferior products attractive using rip-off designs and false packaging.
- Sales experts who hammer flat the feet of plucked chickens in order to get rid of them by selling them as ducks.

For a country that still has party followers advocating a mentality of having dogs and children on leads and forbidding people to tread on the grass, its reputation for innovative leaps and lateral thinkers is purely pretentious. The Intention, the inspiration is the creative factor, not the computer as an extractor of variations or generator of chance. Design requires the ability to visualise in an intense and impartial way. Intense visualising results - concentrated, determined, untiring, diligent and careful – and creates discernment. The enjoyment of taking risks and the courage to evaluate our own capabilities correctly will bring about decisions with a natural accuracy. In the prenatal nine months, we still inevitably make good decisions with our gut. Some people stick at it all their lives.

The design scene is »value pluralistic« which is a better word for clueless. Form still follows function. And in most cases this is also sensible. Even when functions become invisible, disappearing on a chip. The eye, hand, recognition, understanding, comprehension have for a long time not kept pace with the innovative steps and alternating generations of devices in the baby age. Form follows fun or fiction or fantasy. For this our climate is far too moderate.

Typically it is in an area with the least scope for innovation that the maddest, most liberating ideas are being presented: in typography. What a surprise. Here, unfortunately, we have rules which have been tested on our eyes, reading habits, and the form of letters, which have not changed – that is they have been preserved – since Gutenberg. We have become rather more superficial, more impatient and more harassed. Only the production of texts has become highly accelerated, not our ability to see and to understand. The adept on the tracks of Neville Brody, David Carson, Tibor Kalman follow them awkwardly and timidly. We are not able to do such things particularly well.

When the C_d amount in car design stipulated a reduction of air resistance for the sake of jelly babies sucked into smooth, round shapes, and when everything had the same boring look, Rolls Royce continued to show, unimpressed, its angular, creased look. The design of the cockpit was characterised in a brilliant meeting as being »confused, unmethodical and beautiful«. This design deficit did not result in a series of accidents or recall actions (also, the owner also hardly sat at the steering wheel himself).

We will continue to live in very different circumstances: the soft, misty and abstract pushes itself increasingly further and deeper into the more concrete, tangible and visible. The incomprehensible, produced by our fingers – with which we always worked until now – on monitors, in data memories, films and programmes is gaining the upper hand. A society with such a scope as ours will no longer concern itself mainly with designing and producing products, or with selling, consuming or collecting, but will devote itself to the profit of experience, knowledge and transfer of information.

In the search for a Theory for »Everything and Everyone« it is once again belief more than knowledge which leads to the deciphering of questions, according to elegant formulae, on the way of the world. We cannot precisely calculate what avalanches are clotted together there due to the perpetual, global feeding in of information, nor when they will be triggered off or which course they will take – as is the way with avalanches.

The design professions will turn away from the creativity of the fine arts towards intelligent understanding and manipulation of free social needs. Our hands do not have to handle anymore, but merely feel and touch. Miniature devices will be controlled through language. The spiritual essence of art will no longer be created manually.

We are leading a life second and third hand, in an increasingly perfect and clever way. Television, internet, electronic entertainment media degenerate the overtaxed ear and eye. Only when we meet in a direct, unpretentious and open manner, can we still believe our own eyes.

I'm finished.
What a surprise. That's what I say.
And now, the weather

LIMAGE DANGEREUSE

Holländische Designagenturen haben die Chance ergriffen, Aufmerksamkeit für Ihre Arbeit in der Kommunikationsbranche zu wecken. Eine Designagentur mit einem äußerst auffälligen Profil ist Limage Dangereuse. In den letzten zehn Jahren hat sich Limage Dangereuse zu einer multidisziplinären Agentur entwickelt, sie gehört zu den größten in der Region um Rotterdam. Limage Dangereuse bietet Design-Dienstleistungen sowohl für kommerzielle wie kulturelle, für Regierungs- und »Non Profit«-Organisationen in den Bereichen Grafikdesign, Illustration, Multimedia (Animationen, Digitale Präsentationen, CD-ROM, Internetanwendungen, incl. Database und Intranet-Anwendungen) sowie in 3D-Design (Messestände, Museografie, Info-Center und Möbeldesign).

Text: Dirk van Ginkel. Mehr Infos: www.limage-dangereuse.nl

LIMAGE DANGEREUSE

Dutch design agencies have seized the opportunity to claim a spot for their profession in the world of commercial communication. A design agency with an utterly distinct voice in that field is Limage Dangereuse. In the course of ten years Limage Dangereuse has developed into a multidisciplinary design agency, that may be ranked among the largest of the district of Rotterdam. Limage Dangereuse carries out for commercial as well as cultural principals and for governmental and non-profit principals design services in the fields of graphic design, illustrations, multi media (animations, digital presentations, CD-ROM, internet applications including database and intranet applications) and 3D-design (design of stands, museum presentations, set-up of information centers and furniture design).

Text: Dirk van Ginkel. More information: www. limage-dangereuse.nl

Grand Prix

Grand Prix

Father Business

Ausgangspunkt für die Internetanwendung »Father Business« war die Idee, daß Father Business die Homepage ist und die Homepage nichts anderes beinhaltet als die »Arbeit des Vaters«: eine virtuelle Person, die Informationen unter einem persönlichen Eintrag sammelt. Und genauso wie jede Person in ihrer Kommunikation durch Flexibilität und einen gewissen Grad an Anpassung charakterisiert ist, bietet die Homepage ebensolche Möglichkeiten.

Zuerst wird der Besucher aufgefordert, eine Anzahl von persönlichen und geschmacksorientierten Aussagen zu machen, die ihn virtuell repräsentieren sollen. Dann besucht man Father Business, und durch die vorherigen Angaben verändert sich Father Business so, daß es dem Besucher gefällt: Die Farben wechseln (von »hip« zu »sophisticated«), Ton und Musik werden angepaßt (von Pop zu klassischer Musik) und ein paar Illustrationen/Animationen kommen hinzu.

Die Auswahl des Besuchers wird sichtbar in einem Avatar, (eine virtuelle Person) in Form eines Ikons (Puppe). Dieser Avatar kommt an verschiedenen Stellen der Homepage immer wieder vor: als Besucher oder als Ikon vor entsprechenden Eintragungen ins Gästebuch. Dies erscheint auch in der Datenbank unter Name, Adresse und Stadt, so daß dieses Ikon z.B. auch beim Ausdruck auf ein T-Shirt direkt vor dem Namen ausgedruckt wird. Auf diesem Weg vermischen sich die virtuelle Welt von Father Business und die reale Welt immer mehr.

Father Business

Point of departure for the internet application of Father Business was the idea that Father Business is the site and that the site is father business. A virtual intellect / person that recruits and informs on a personal title. And just as any person is characterised in his communications by flexibility and a certain degree of adjustment, the site will also have these features.

First of all the site asks the visitor to make himself known by means of making a number of taste and person bound choices, which will represent the visitor on the site in a virtual way. One is paying a visit to father business. Father business will adjust itself to a certain extent to please the visitor. The colours change (from hip to sophisticated), the sound and the music are adjusted (from pop to classical) and a number of illustrations/ animations will adjust themselves.

The choices of the visitor will be made concrete in an avatar (a virtual representation) in the form of an icon (a puppet). This avatar will return in various places in the site. As the visitor, or as icon in the case of entries in the guests' book. This is also added to the database of data concerning name, address and town, so that, for instance, this puppet is printed on the label on the T-shirt in front of the name. In this way the virtual world of father business and the real world will merge.

FATHER BUSINESS—
WWW.FATHERBUSI-
NESS.NL

4/1999

CLIENT
Spyros, Zeist,
The Netherlands

DESIGN
Limage Dangereuse,
Rotterdam,
The Netherlands
Idea, Design, Techniques:
Limage Dangereuse
Rotterdam
Brand development:
Bert Rorije
Illustrations/Animations: Limage Dangereuse Rotterdam
Sound: Limage
Dangereuse Rotterdam/
Mark Moget
Text: Astrid van den Berg

JUNIOR PRIZE
JUNIORPREIS

Mit dem erstmalig ausgeschriebenen »Juniorpreis« sollen herausragende Diplom- und Abschlußarbeiten ausgezeichnet werden. Teilnehmen können alle Studierenden aus den Fachbereichen Foto-, Grafik- und Kommunikationsdesign. Verliehen wurde der Preis an die Diplomarbeit »Wenn die Nacht kein Ende nimmt...« von Tamara Narolski, Absolventin der Fachhochschule Düsseldorf. Zu Idee und Konzept Ihrer Diplomarbeit, einem eindrucksvoll gestalteten und aufwendig verarbeiteten Buch mit besonderer Falttechnik schreibt sie:

»'Wenn die Nacht kein Ende nimmt...' ist ein Buchprojekt, das über die Krankheit Schizophrenie informieren soll. Es verdeutlicht die Situation der an Schizophrenie Erkrankten und deren Angehörigen, zeigt einerseits die öffentliche Meinung zu dem Thema und andererseits die Gefühle und Gedanken des Betroffenen. Entsprechend dieser Idee besteht das Buch aus zwei einzelnen Buchabschnitten, die räumlich voneinander getrennt bzw. versetzt sind. Sie gliedern sich in ein 'Außenbuch' und ein 'Innenbuch'. Das 'Außenbuch' zeigt auf, wie die Gesellschaft die Schizophrenie sieht, wie sie mit diesem Thema umgeht und mit welchen Schwierigkeiten Erkrankte und Angehörige konfrontiert werden. Das 'Innenbuch' spiegelt die Gefühlswelt des Menschen in einer Schizophrenie wieder. Es beschreibt Symptome und läßt teilhaben an den Gefühlen von Erkrankten und Angehörigen.«

Tamara Narolski, geboren 1973, studierte nach ihrer Ausbildung zur Gestaltungstechnischen Assistentin Visuelle Kommunikation an der Fachhochschule Düsseldorf. Seit 1993 arbeitet sie als Grafikerin für verschiedene Agenturen, ab Januar 2000 als Junior Art Directorin bei der BMZ!FCA Werbeagentur GmbH & Co.KG in Düsseldorf.

The »Junior Prize« which is being awarded for the first time is to recognise outstanding degree work. Participants entering can be students from the areas of photographic design, graphic design and communication design. The Prize was awarded for the degree work »When the night never ends...« by Tamara Narolski, a graduate from the University of Düsseldorf. On the idea and concept of her book, which has been designed and worked on impressively with special folding techniques, she writes:

»'When the night never ends...' is a book project which is aimed to inform people about the illness schizophrenia. It clarifies the situation that schizophrenics and their relatives are in. On the one hand, it shows public opinion on the subject and, on the other hand, it shows the feelings and thoughts of those affected. This idea is thus shown in the book which consists of two single parts which are separated or staggered spatially. They are divided in an 'Outer Book' and an 'Inner Book.' The 'Outer Book' shows how society sees schizophrenia, how society deals with the topic and the difficulties that those affected and their relatives are confronted with. The 'Inner Book' mirrors the feelings of those suffering from the illness. It describes symptoms and allows one to be part of the feelings of schizophrenics and their relatives.«

Tamara Narolski, born in 1973, studied Visual Communication at the University of Düsseldorf following her training as a Technical Design Assistant. She has been working as a Graphic Designer for various agencies since 1993 and will start as Junior Art Director with BMZ!FCA Werbeagentur GmbH & Co.KG in Düsseldorf in January 2000.

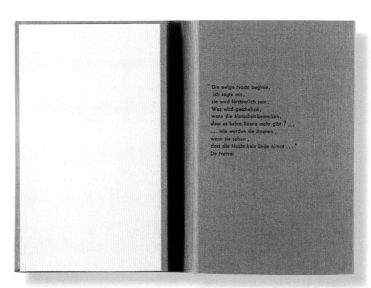
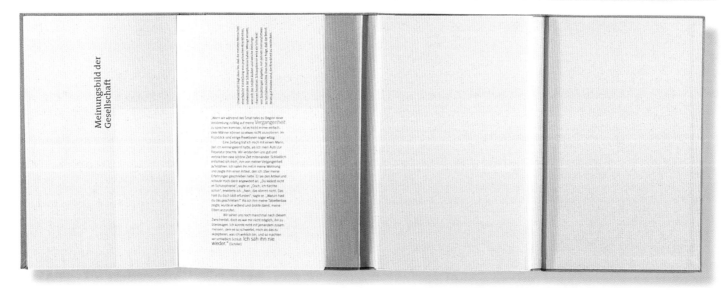

WENN DIE NACHT KEIN ENDE NIMMT... [EIN BUCH ZUM THEMA SCHIZOPHRENIE]
1999
DESIGN Tamara Narolski, Essen

HÖCHSTE DESIGNQUALITÄT

Highest Design Quality

Mit der Ehrenauszeichnung für Höchste Designqualität prämiert die international besetzte Jury Arbeiten, die außergewöhnlich hohen Ansprüchen an die gestalterische Qualität, an den Innovationsgrad, an die Ästhetik, den Gehalt und die Prägnanz entsprechen. Die Auszeichnung vergibt das Design Zentrum Nordrhein Westfalen an die maximal drei besten Arbeiten der einzelnen Produktgruppen. Die insgesamt acht Gruppen umfassen Arbeiten aus den Bereichen Juniorpreis, Werbung, Unternehmenskommunikation, Produktkommunikation, Fernsehen und elektronische Medien, Kultur und Sport, Verlagswesen, Multimedia. Unter 2.327 Einsendungen wählten die Juroren Hans P. Brandt, Christof Gassner, Günter Gerhard Lange, Uwe Loesch, Jutta Nachtwey, Iris Utikal, Kurt Weidemann, Jean Widmer und Prof. Peter Zec 27 Arbeiten aus, denen sie Höchste Designqualität bescheinigten. 24 dieser prämierten Arbeiten sind hier dokumentiert.

With the honours award for the Highest Design Quality, the international jury is awarding work which has an unusually high standard of design quality with focus on the degree of innovation, aesthetics, content and succintness. The award is being given by the Design Zentrum Nordrhein Westfalen to a maximum of the three best works in single product groups. A total of eight groups consist of work from the areas of Junior Prize, Advertising, Corporate Communications, Product Communications, Television and Electronic Media, Culture and Sport, Publishing and Multimedia. From the 2,327 entries received, the jurors Hans P. Brandt, Christof Gassner, Günter Gerhard Lange, Uwe Loesch, Jutta Nachtwey, Iris Utikal, Kurt Weidemann, Jean Widmer and Prof. Peter Zec have selected 27 pieces of work which represented the Highest Design Quality. 24 of the works awarded are documented here.

TV-Spot »Schiessbude« 12/1998	
Client WWF Deutschland, Frankfurt	
Design Ogilvy & Mather, Frankfurt Johannes Krempl Patrick They	
Production Company Neue Sentimental Film, Frankfurt Regie: Tom Gläser	

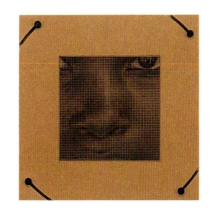

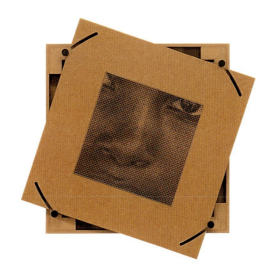

ITINERAIRE DES
DROITS DE L'HOMME

1998

CLIENT
Atelier Roger Pfund
Communication
Visuelle SA, Carouge
Suisse

DESIGN
Atelier Roger Pfund
Communication
Visuelle Sa., Carouge
Suisse
Roger Pfund

HdK_

Hochschule der Künste Berlin
Bildende Kunst Gestaltung Musik Darstellende Kunst

Hochschule der Künste Berlin
Bildende Kunst Gestaltung Musik Darstellende Kunst

Hochschule der Künste Berlin
Bildende Kunst Gestaltung Musik Darstellende Kunst

Hochschule der Künste Berlin
Bildende Kunst Gestaltung Musik Darstellende Kunst

Hochschule der Künste Berlin
Bildende Kunst Gestaltung Musik Darstellende Kunst

Visuelles Erscheinungsbild für die Hochschule der Künste Berlin [Juniorpreis]
5/1998
Design Tina Bühling, Berlin

Hochschule der Künste Berlin   Fakultätsverwaltung
Bildende Kunst Gestaltung Musik Darstellende Kunst

Hochschule der Künste Berlin Postfach 12 6720 D 10595 Berlin

Jan Tomas Mustermann   Hardenbergstrasse 33
Beispielstrasse 22   D 10 623 Berlin

10885 Berlin   Zeichen VL
                                         Bearbeitung Frau Muster
                                         Telefon 030 3185 2251
                                         Telefax 030 3185 2252
                                         e-mail vl@hdk-berlin.de

Sehr geehrte Damen und Herren,   10 12 97

dieses ist ein Blindtext, der keine inhaltliche Bedeutung
hat. Aber durch ihn können Sie sehen, wie der Briefbogen
beschrieben aussieht.

Denn wann sieht man schon einen unbeschriebenen Briefbogen.
Dieses ist ein Blindtext, der keine inhaltliche Bedeutung
hat. Aber durch ihn können Sie sehen, wie der Briefbogen
beschrieben aussieht. Denn wann sieht man schon einen
unbeschriebenen Briefbogen.

Dieses ist ein Blindtext, der keine inhaltliche Bedeutung
hat. Aber durch ihn können Sie sehen, wie der Briefbogen
beschrieben aussieht. Denn wann sieht man schon einen
unbeschriebenen Briefbogen.

Mit freundlichen Grüßen

Hochschule der Künste Berlin
Bildende Kunst Gestaltung Musik Darstellende Kunst

Prof. Dr. Henning Schreyer
Dekan
Ernst Reuter Platz 10
D 10587 Berlin
Telefon 030 3185 2447
Telefax 030 3185 2448

Bankverbindung
Postbank Berlin
Bankleitzahl 100 100 10
Kontonummer 15 58 106
Technische Universität Berlin
Hinweis „HdK Bln"

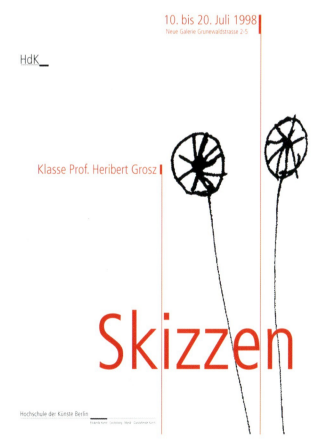

ELEVEN22.
DIE NEUE SICHT
DER DINGE.

6/1998

CLIENT
USM U. Schärer
Söhne AG,
Münsingen, Schweiz

DESIGN
Scholz & Volkmer
GmbH, Wiesbaden

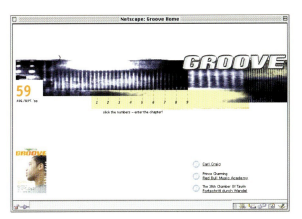
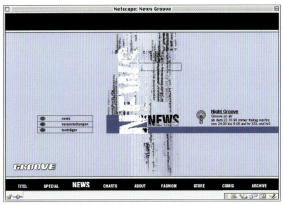

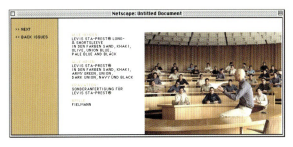

GROOVE
1999
Client GROOVE Musikmagazin, Frankfurt
Design Neue Digitale, Frankfurt Andreas Gahlert Olaf Czeschner Programmierer: Christian Gelbach PR: Pascale Brinkmann

5 Arbeitsproben
Volume 2
7/1999
Client
Atelier Beinert & Sonner, München
Design
Atelier Beinert & Sonner, München
Wolfgang Beinert
Carolin Sonner

Geschäftsbericht	
Kabel New Media	
6/1999	
Client	
Kabel New Media, Hamburg	
Design	
Factor Design AG, Hamburg	

Portfolio Schumacher Gebler
7/1999
Client   Römerturm Feinstpapiere, Frechen
Design   Factor Design AG, Hamburg

VORWERK KONZERN-GESCHÄFTSBERICHT 1998
1998
CLIENT Vorwerk & Co., Wuppertal
DESIGN Hermann Michels, Wuppertal

Home Sweet home

12/1998

Client
Valkenburg Printers
Echt/Polka Design,
Roermond
The Netherlands

Design
Polka Design,
Roermond,
The Netherlands
Joep Pohlen

MEDITATION IN WORTEN UND TÖNEN
7/1998
CLIENT   Münchener Hypothekenbank eG, München
DESIGN   Atelier Beinert & Sonner, München   Wolfgang Beinert   Carolin Sonner

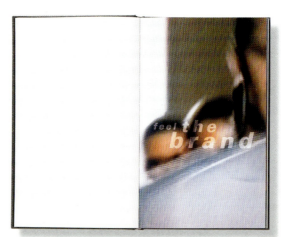

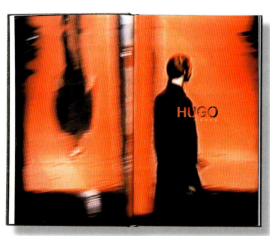

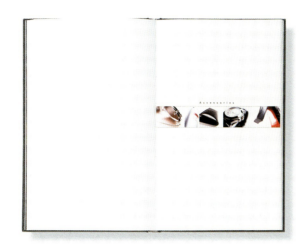

Hugo Boss
Geschäftsbericht
1999
Client
Hugo Boss AG, Metzingen
Design
Peter Schmidt Studios GmbH, Hamburg
Benjamin Klöck,
Jan Klaas Mahler,
Norbert Möller

Spheros-Buch	
1998	
Client	Loewe Opta GmbH, Kronach
Design	Leonhardt & Kern Werbung GmbH, Stuttgart

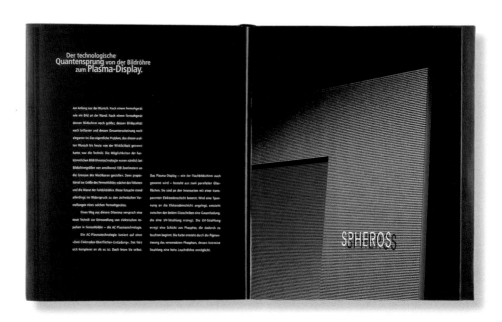

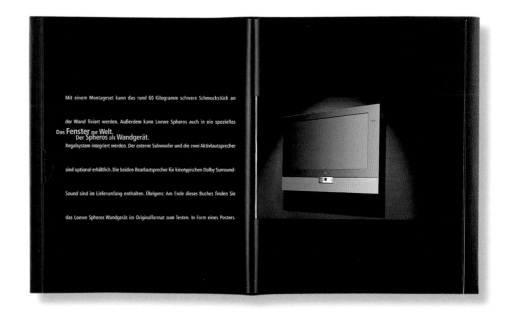

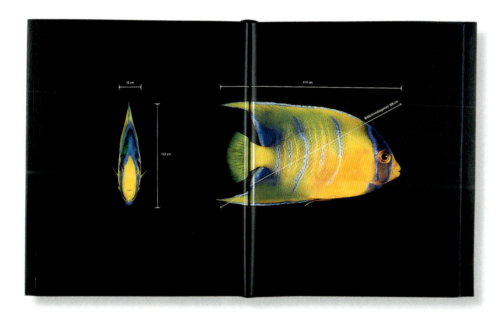
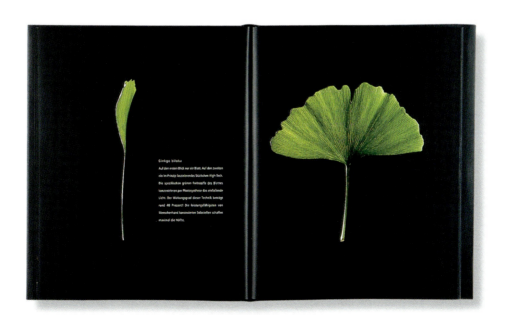

SAVE [RED SERIES]

8/1998

DESIGN
Nippon Design Center Inc., Tokyo, Japan
Kazumasa Nagai

SAVE
[YELLOW SERIES]

8/1998

DESIGN
Nippon Design Center
Inc., Tokyo, Japan
Kazumasa Nagai

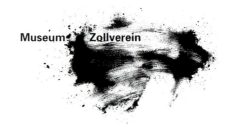

SIGNET MUSEUM ZOLLVEREIN	
1999	
CLIENT Bauhütte Zeche Zollverein Schacht XII GmbH, Essen	
DESIGN verb Agentur für Kommunikations- design GmbH, Essen	

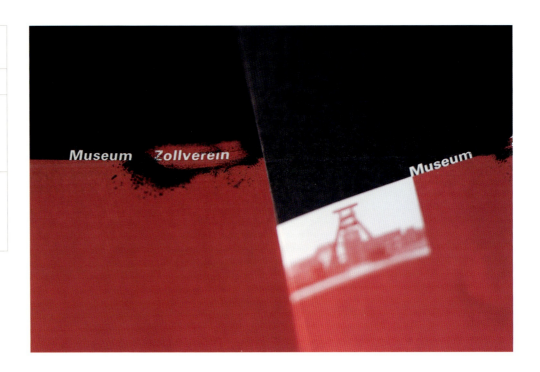

Strandgut	
[Juniorpreis]	
1999	
Design	
Christian Tönsmann, Hamburg	

HOLLYWOOD
AAN DE MAAS

11/1998

DESIGN
Proforma Graphic
Designers & Consul-
tance, Rotterdam,
The Netherlands
Marisa Klaster
Jeroen Berg

KUNSTHALLE DÜSSELDORF, RODTSCHENKO AUSSTELLUNG

1998

CLIENT
Kunsthalle Düsseldorf

DESIGN
Rempen & Partner:
Das Design Büro,
Düsseldorf
Stefan Baggen

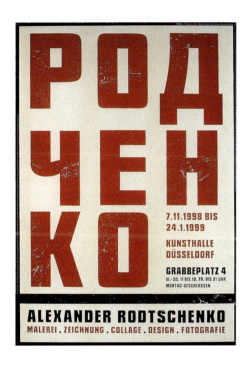
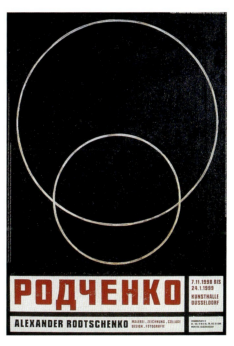

MAZZINI/PAYER
4/1998
DESIGN
Almut Riebe, Frankfurt

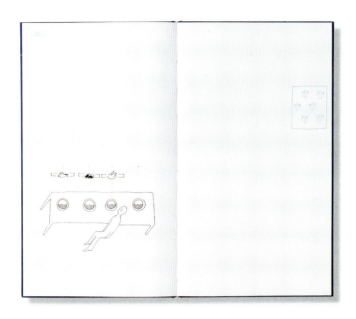

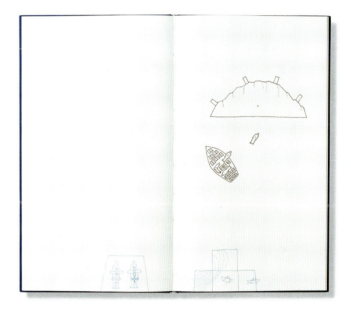
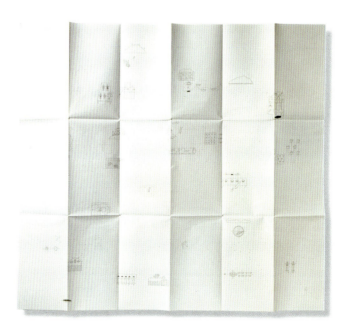

Nez Du Café
1997
Client
Editions Jean Lenoir, Carnoux en Provence, France
Design
Atelier Roger Pfund Communication Visuelle SA, Carouge Suisse
Roger Pfund

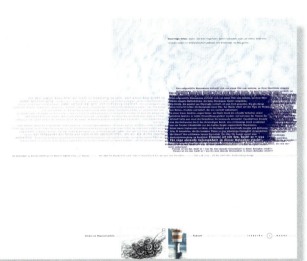
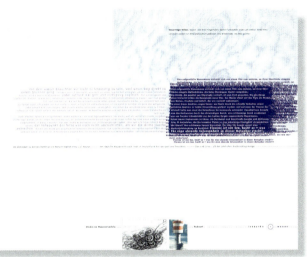
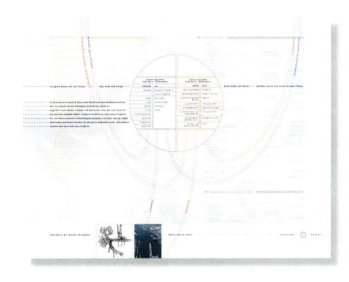
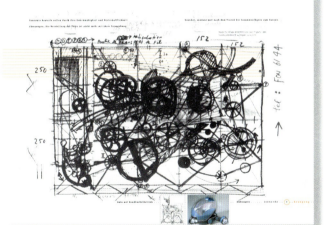

...SEHEN...ERFINDEN
[JUNIORPREIS]

1998

CLIENT
Staatliche Akademie der Bildenden Künste, Stuttgart

DESIGN
Anja Wesner, München

Wild Wild West
6/1999
Client Warner Brothers (Barry Sonnenfeld) Burbank, USA
Design Imaginary Forces, Hollywood, USA

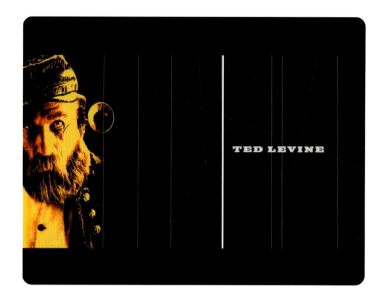
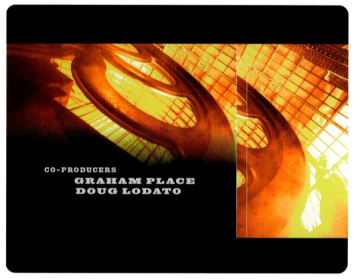

Non-Art-Neujahrsgabe an Kunden, Lieferanten und Freunde
1999
Client   Burkhardt Leitner constructiv, Stuttgart
Design   Burkhardt Leitner constructiv, Stuttgart

WERBUNG [Hohe Designqualität]
Anzeigen Kampagnen Plakate Verkaufsbroschüren Kataloge

ADVERTISING [High Design Quality]
Printed ads Campaigns Posters Prospectuses Sales brochures Catalogs

Schaltsysteme für die Industrie Gesamtkatalog

4/1999

Client
K.A. Schmersal GmbH & Co., Industrieschaltgeräte, Wuppertal

Design
Büro Longjaloux GmbH, Wuppertal
Stephan Preuß
Stephan Degens
Dirk Longjaloux

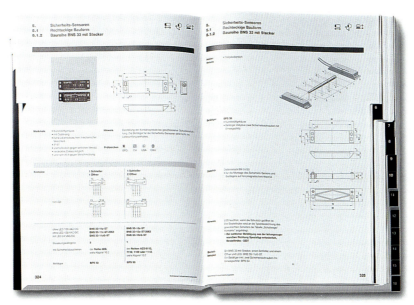

TV-Spot »Wenn der Vater mit dem Sohne«

12/1998

Client
SWR Baden-Baden, Baden-Baden

Design
Ogilvy & Mather Frankfurt
Johannes Krempl
Patrick They

Production Company
Neue Sentimental Film, Berlin
Regie: Nico Beyer

SPIRIT
2/1999
CLIENT Ruckstuhl AG, Langenthal, Suisse
DESIGN P'INC. AG, Langenthal, Suisse Urs Hug

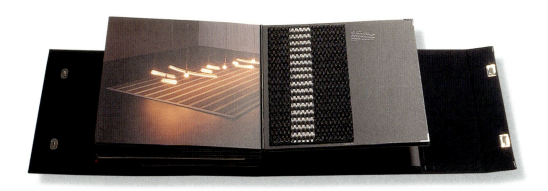

LOEWE SPHEROS ANZEIGE

1998

CLIENT
Loewe Opta GmbH, Kronach

DESIGN
Leonhardt & Kern Werbung GmbH, Stuttgart
Joachim Silber

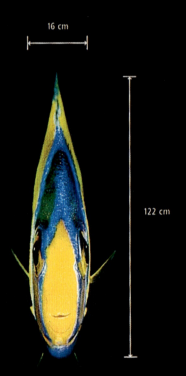

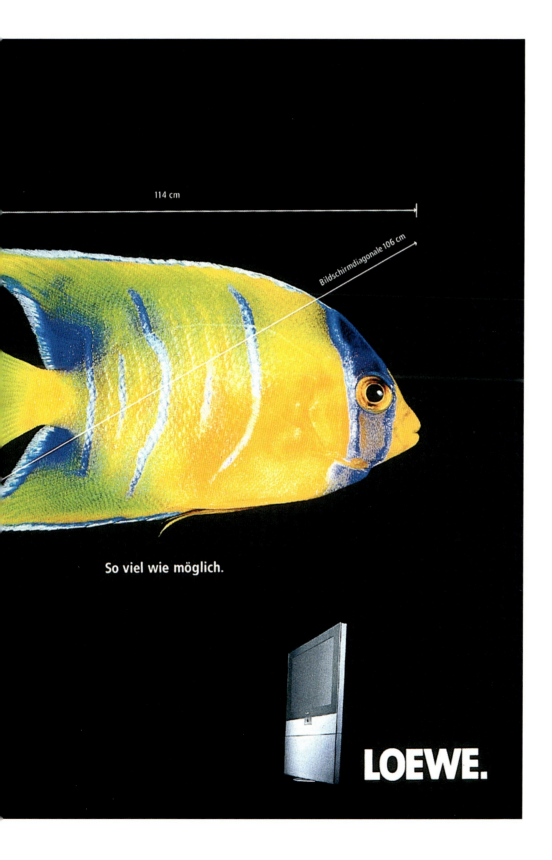

LOTHAR BERTRAMS, PORTFOLIO 1

3/1999

CLIENT
Lothar Bertrams, Stuttgart

DESIGN
Büro Uebele
Visuelle Kommunikation, Stuttgart
Jutta Boxheimer
Susanne Fritsch
Andreas Uebele

CLIC-BOX
9/1998
Client Burkhardt Leitner constructiv, Stuttgart
Design Fleischmann & Kirsch, Stuttgart

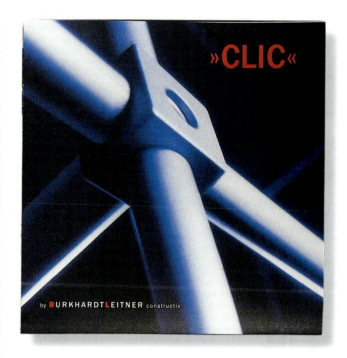

VIVA ZWEI-ANZEIGE

7/1999

CLIENT
Viva Fernsehen
GmbH & Co. KG, Köln

DESIGN
BOROS GmbH,
Wuppertal
Christian Boros

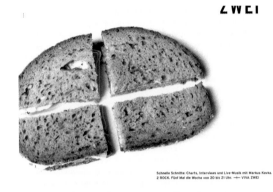

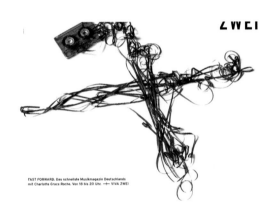

Rosso Katalog
7/1999
Client Nimbus GmbH, Stuttgart
Design Büro Uebele Visuelle Kommunikation, Stuttgart Andreas Uebele

KRIEGSSPIELE
[JUNIORPREIS]

6/1998

DESIGN
Oliver Leichsenring,
Naumburg

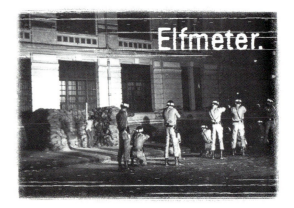

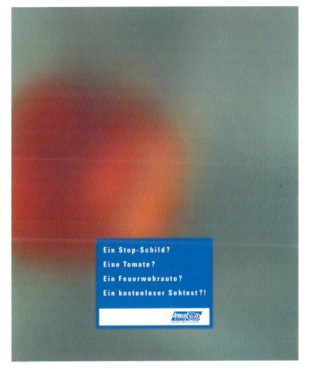

Unscharf	
3/1999	
Client	Apollo Optik GmbH & Co. KG, Schwabach
Design	JvM an der Isar, München

King Kong / Godzilla

2/1999

Client
Sixt GmbH & Co.
Autovermietung KG,
Pullach

Design
JvM an der Isar,
München

Siegestor	
4/1998	
Client	Sixt GmbH & Co. Autovermietung KG, Pullach
Design	JvM an der Isar, München

Idiom	
1999	
Client Emery Vincent Design Victoria, Australia	
Design Emery Vincent Design team, Victoria, Australia	

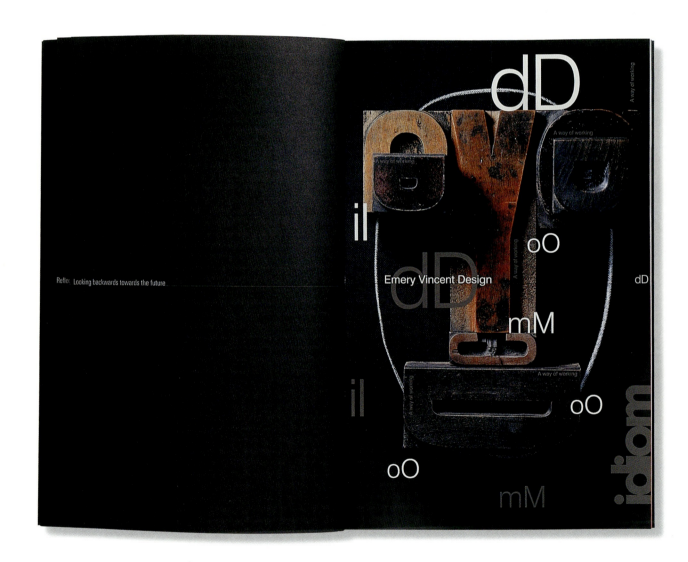

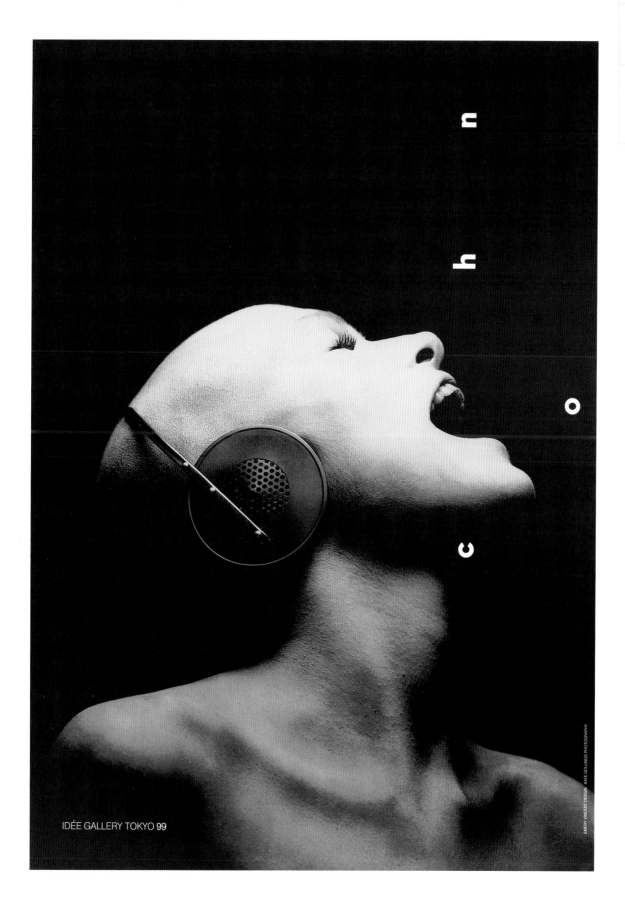

Susan Cohn
Poster

1999

Client
Workshop 3000, Melborne, Australia

Design
Emery Vincent Design team, Victoria, Australia

JANUS

1/1999
3/1999

CLIENT
Foote, Cone & Belding (Janus), San Francisco, USA

DESIGN
Imaginary Forces, Hollywood, USA

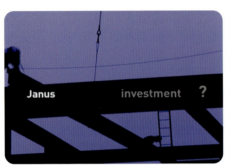

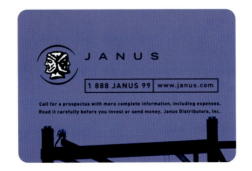

DF TYPE
MAILING FÜR DIE NEUE TYPE RIALTO
1999
DESIGN
df Type, Texing, Austria Lui Karner Giovanni de Faccio

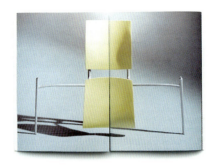

PHILIPPE STARCK FOR CASSINA	
1998	
CLIENT	Cassina, Milano, Italy
DESIGN	Michael·Nash Associates, London, Great Britain Anthony Michael Stephanie Nash
PHOTOGRAPHY	Matthew Donaldson

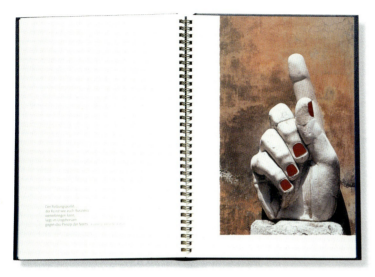
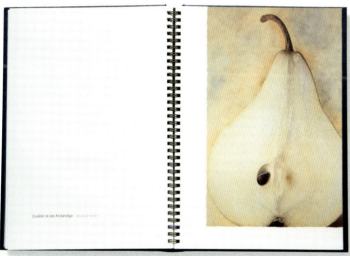
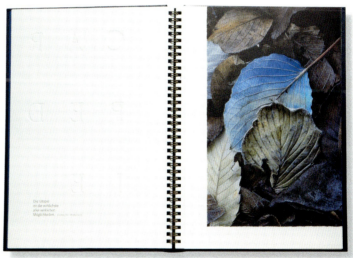
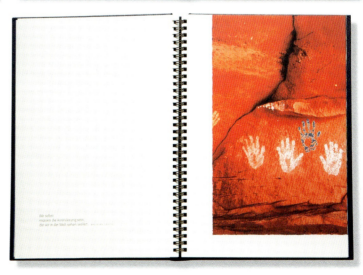

NEUES SEHEN

10/1998

CLIENT
Arbeitskreis
Prägefoliendruck e.V.,
Göppingen

DESIGN
Hubert Minsch
Kommunikations-
design, Waldstetten
Hubert Minsch

TÜVIT-
IMAGEPROSPEKT

1998

CLIENT
TÜV Informations-
technik GmbH, Essen

DESIGN
Loermann & Schrödter
Werbeagentur GmbH,
Essen
Gottfried Loermann
Dieter Schrödter
Matthias Löcker

Empfang zum Wechsel	
1998	
Client	Bertelsmann AG, Gütersloh
Design	Bertelsmann AG, Gütersloh Stephanie Gesing

Bertelsmann in Transition	
1998	
Client	Bertelsmann AG, Gütersloh
Design	Bertelsmann AG, Gütersloh Stephanie Gesing

UNSER LEITBILD

6/1999

CLIENT
Die Sparkasse Bremen, Bremen

DESIGN
in(corporate, Bremen

ökologischen Grundsätzen.

Wir orientieren uns an

Ökologische Gesichtspunkte fließen in unsere geschäftspolitischen Entscheidungen ein.
Wir unterstützen ökologische Projekte, Vorhaben und Initiativen.

Die Verwirklichung von Umweltschutz ist für uns ein kontinuierlicher Prozeß. So sind ökologische Gesichtspunkte Bestandteil unserer geschäftspolitischen Entscheidungen geworden. Und damit aus guten Vorsätzen Maßnahmen werden, haben wir Umweltleitlinien erarbeitet. Damit verpflichten wir uns beispielsweise, die gesetzlichen Bestimmungen als Mindestanforderungen zu verstehen und ein höheres Maß an Umweltschutz anzustreben. Regelmäßig geben wir uns Rechenschaft über den Stand des Umweltschutzes in der Sparkasse Bremen.
Unsere Mitarbeiterinnen und Mitarbeiter informieren wir über Umweltaspekte. Darüber hinaus wollen wir dieses Thema in unsere hausinternen Bildungsmaßnahmen integrieren. Selbstverständlich setzen wir Energie, Wasser und Verbrauchsgüter so sparsam wie möglich ein und berücksichtigen die Lebenszeit verwendeter Produkte sowie deren umweltgerechte Entsorgung.

Durch die voranschreitende Datenvernetzung aller Arbeitsplätze führen wir die Vorbereitungen zu einem weitgehend papierlosen Büro weiter. Der zentrale Einkauf bewertet die Büromaterialien ökologisch und tauscht Produkte nach diesem System aus. Stoffe, die der Gefahrstoffverordnung unterliegen, werden durch alternative Produkte ersetzt.
Unsere ökologische Selbstverpflichtung bezieht sich auch auf das Bauen und Renovieren. So verpflichten wir unsere Vertragspartner, umweltfreundliche Materialien zu verwenden. Die Umsetzung neuer Erkenntnisse wird in unserem Hause kontinuierlich verfolgt.

Windpark Blockland

WWF

Die Sparkasse Bremen trägt mit ihrer Kompetenz als Finanzdienstleister wesentlich zur Stärkung des regionalen Wirtschaftsraumes bei. Zusätzlich nehmen wir unsere Verantwortung als bedeutendes Wirtschaftsunternehmen bewußt wahr und fördern damit den Standort Bremen.
Als Arbeitgeber für über 2.300 Mitarbeiterinnen und Mitarbeiter, mit einem Steueraufkommen von mehr als 50 Mio DM pro Jahr und als Ausbilder von 160 jungen Menschen leisten wir hier einen wesentlichen Beitrag.
Darüber hinaus ist die Sparkasse als Auftraggeber, Einkäufer und Bauherr ein wichtiger Partner des Bremer Handwerks und des Einzelhandels.

Gewinnerzielung ist dabei für uns kein Selbstzweck. Für die Sparkasse Bremen als verantwortungsbewußtes regionales Unternehmen sind Kostenkontrolle und Ertragsstärke unverzichtbar. Auf der Grundlage von Wirtschaftlichkeit und Rentabilität wird ein erheblicher Teil der im Wettbewerb erzielten Erträge wieder zur Verbesserung der Standortbedingungen in Bremen eingesetzt.

Wir unterstützen ressourcenschonendes Wirtschaften und die Erhaltung der Umwelt als wichtigste Zukunftsaufgabe. Wir fördern soziales Engagement im Interesse des Gemeinwohls, die Erhaltung kultureller Bausubstanz, Kunst, Kultur sowie Wissenschaft ebenso wie den Spitzen- und Breitensport. Über ihre berufliche Tätigkeit hinaus sind viele Mitarbeiterinnen und Mitarbeiter ehrenamtlich tätig.
Unser Engagement ist vielfältig und weitreichender als lediglich finanzielle Zuwendung und verbessert so die Lebensqualität vor Ort.

Mittelstandsforum

Bremer Unternehmensbeteiligungsgesellschaft (BUG)

Sponsoring

Wir sind uns unserer Verantwortung als bedeutendes Wirtschaftsunternehmen bewußt.
Wir fördern die Standortqualität zum Wohl der Menschen.
Wir initiieren und fördern wirtschaftliche und gesellschaftliche Entwicklungen.

Wir arbeiten für die Lebensqualität der Menschen in der Region – heute und morgen.

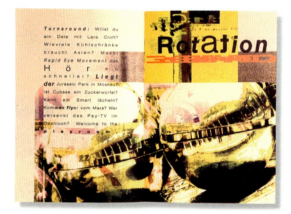

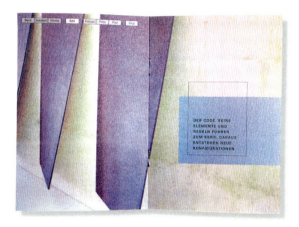

DECADES

1/1999

CLIENT
Füsser_Schmidt.
Thomas Füsser,
Geli Schmidt,
Hamburg
Apitzsch Proof GmbH,
Hamburg
Büttenpapierfabrik
Gmund GmbH und
Co. KG

DESIGN
Füsser_Schmidt.
Thomas Füsser,
Geli Schmidt,
Hamburg

Anwaltskanzlei Zuck und Quaas

7/1999

Client
Anwaltskanzlei Zuck und Quaas, Stuttgart

Design
Peter Horlacher
Büro für Gestaltung, Stuttgart
Peter Horlacher

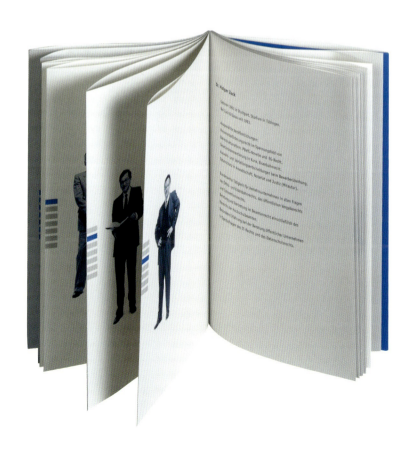

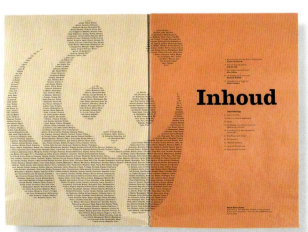

JAARVERSLAG WNF

1998

CLIENT
Wereld Natuur Fonds,
Zeist, The Netherlands

DESIGN
Samenwerkende
Ontwerpers,
Amsterdam, The
Nethetlands
André Toet

Maas ci	
1999	
Client	Juwelier Maas, Stuttgart
Design	Hebe Werbung & Design, Leonberg Reiner Hebe

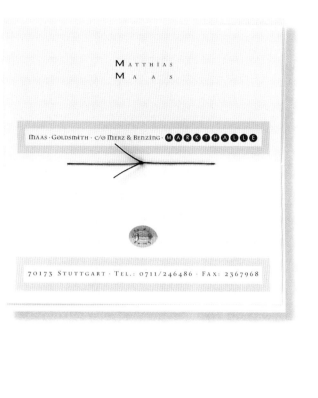
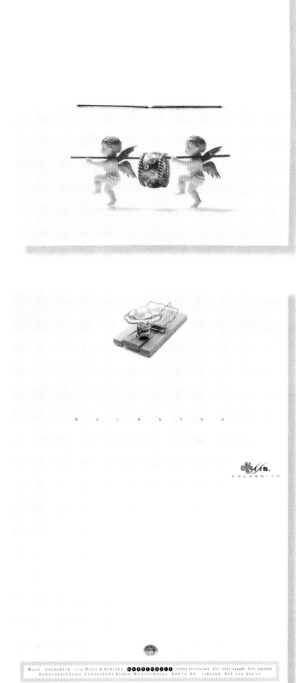

INTEGRATA TRAINING AG GESCHÄFTSBERICHT 1998

1999

CLIENT
Integrata Training AG, Tübingen

DESIGN
Bilek & Co Werbeagentur GWA, Stuttgart

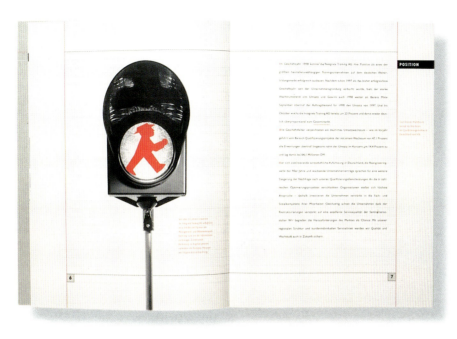

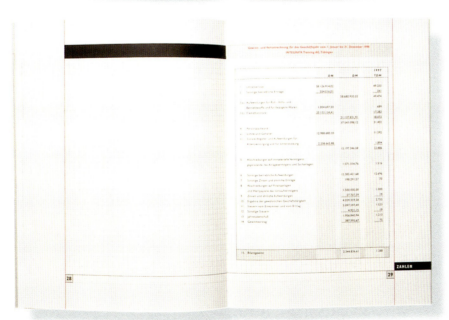

Imagebroschüre futur 3	
6/1999	
Client	futur 3, Saarbrücker Zentrum für integrierte Zukunftskonzepte, Saarbrücken
Design	Maksimovic & Partners, Saarbrücken AD: Ivica Maksimovic, Patrick Bittner Graphics: Patrick Bittner Photography: Isabel Bach Typographie: Patrick Bittner

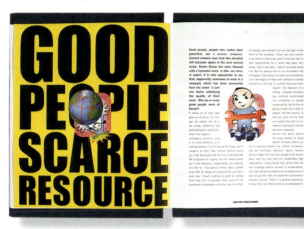

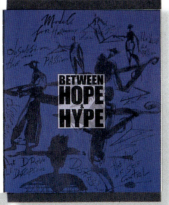

Secon Group
1998
Client
Secon Group, Amsterdam, The Netherlands
Design
Samenwerkende Ontwerpers, Amsterdam, The Netherlands André Toet

Medien	
2/1999	
Client	BTM Berner Tageblatt Medien AG, Bern, Suisse
Design	Külling + Partner Identity, Zürich, Suisse

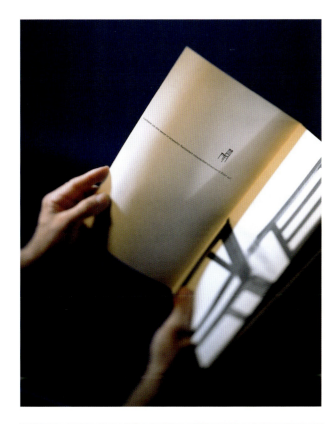
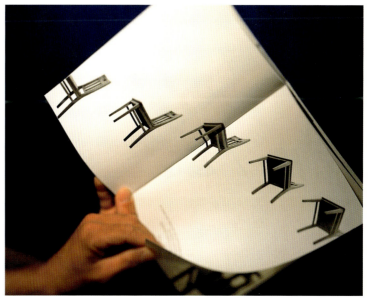
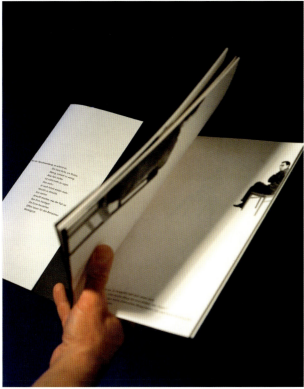

FREISTELLEN
1/1999
DESIGN
Lutz Krause, Guido Kasper, Konstanz

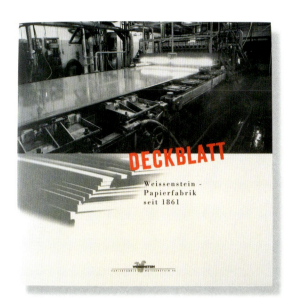

DECKBLATT, WEISSENSTEIN...	
1997	
CLIENT	
Papierfabrik Weissenstein, Pforzheim	
DESIGN	
INTRO Marketing, Pforzheim	
Conception, Text: Michael Mürle	
Graphic-Design: Thomas Ochs	
Photography: Harald Koch	

1861, als die noch junge Papierindustrie turbulente Entwicklungen durchlebte und der Begriff "Luxuspapiere" in Fachkreisen als Synonym für neue Märkte kursierte, wurde die Papierfabrik Weissenstein gegründet.

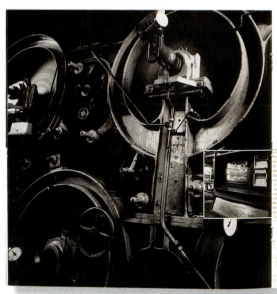

Auch die Produktivität der Mitarbeiter wird nicht im Tonnen-Takt gemessen. Spezialisten, erfahrene Fachkräfte sind gefragt. Leute mit Liebe zum Produkt. Menschen, die sich ein Stück Tradition und den Berufsstolz der alten „Papyrer" bewahrt haben.

„Abseits von aller Welt, in der Einsamkeit waldreicher Täler, geht der Papyrer seinem Berufe besonderer Art nach."

ABGELEHNT

12/1998

CLIENT
Factor Design AG, Hamburg

DESIGN
Factor Design AG, Hamburg

UNTERNEHMENS-PROFIL CABLECOM

6/1999

CLIENT
Cablecom Holding
AG, Zürich, Suisse

DESIGN
Jaray·Visual Concepts,
Zürich, Suisse
Peter Jaray

ANZEIGENTRENDS·98
1999
CLIENT   Akademie Bildsprache, Hamburg
DESIGN   Büro Hamburg, Hamburg   Régine Thienhaus

IMAGEBROSCHÜRE, GONTARD & METALLBANK AG
1999
CLIENT
Gontard & Metall-Bank Aktiengesellschaft, Frankfurt
DESIGN
Beithan, Heßler Werbeagentur GmbH, Frankfurt

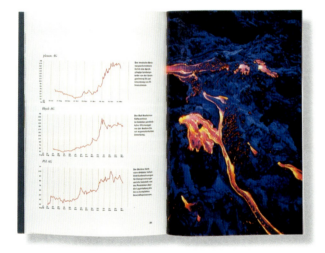

GESCHÄFTSAUSSTATTUNG FÜR SPRICH
2/1999
CLIENT Daniela Müller, Stuttgart
DESIGN KMS, München Petra Kobrow

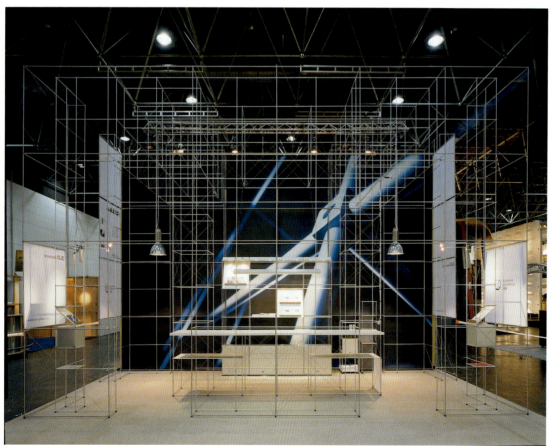

Messeauftritt	
1999	
Client	Burkhardt Leitner constructiv, Stuttgart
Design	Team Burkhardt Leitner constructiv, Stuttgart Fleischmann & Kirsch, Stuttgart

MUSEUM DER DINGE
7/1999
CLIENT
museum der dinge,
berlin
DESIGN
im stall gmbh,
agentur für marken-
und medienkonzepte,
berlin
claudius lazzeroni
dagmar puzberg

ANNUAL REPORT 1998 AMSTERDAM RAI

4/1999

CLIENT
Amsterdam RAI, The Netherlands

DESIGN
Shape bv, Amsterdam, The Netherlands
Hans Versteeg

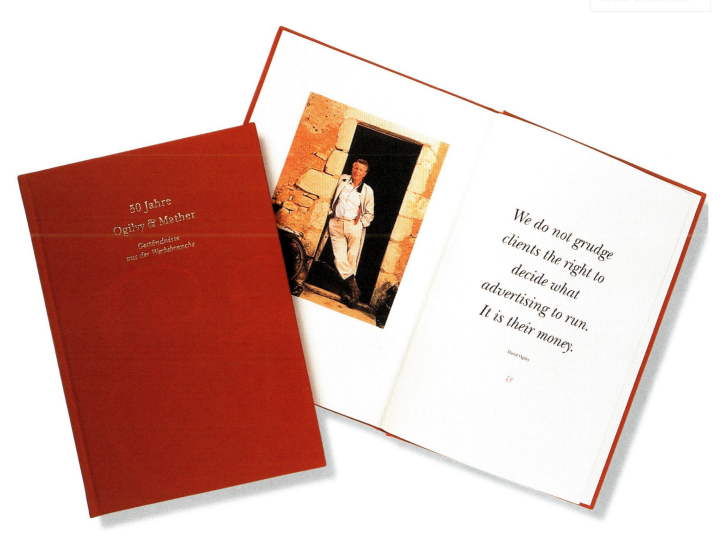

DAS GESTÄNDNISSE-BOOKLET

9/1998

DESIGN
Ogilvy & Mather,
Frankfurt
Lutz Augustin
Lothar S. Leonhard

ANNUAL REPORT
1997
1998
CLIENT
IntroGene, Leiden, The Netherlands
DESIGN
Eric van Casteren ontwerpers, Den Haag, The Netherlands

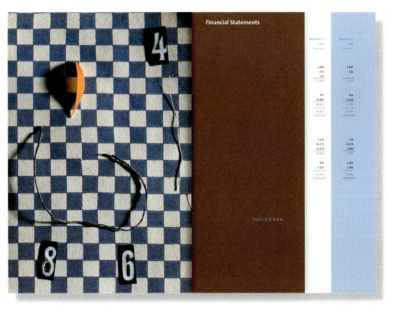

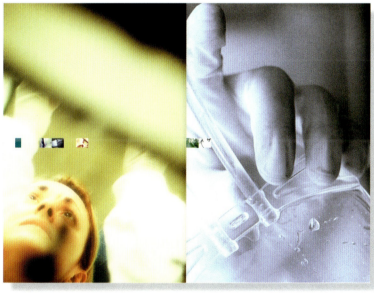

Annual Report 1998	
	1999
Client	IntroGene, Leiden, The Netherlands
Design	Eric van Casteren ontwerpers, Den Haag, The Netherlands

THE SPIRIT OF
SPACELAB

4/1999

CLIENT
DaimlerChrysler
Aerospace Raum-
fahrt-Infrastruktur,
Bremen

DESIGN
Brasilhaus No.8
GmbH, Bremen
Jana Knust
Alexander Held

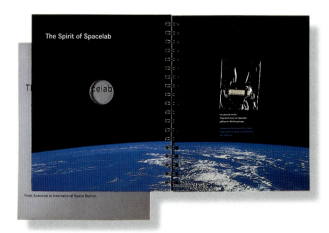

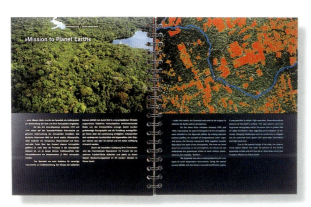

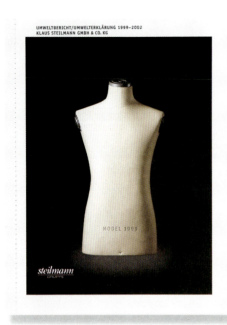
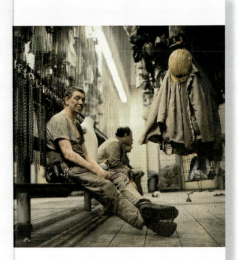

Umweltbericht/ Umwelterklärung 1999-2002	
7/1999	
Client	Klaus Steilmann GmbH & Co. KG, Bochum
Design	Gerk und Krauss, Konzeptionelle Werbung, Bochum Thorsten Gerk Heide Krauss

Vinzentz art in architecture

4/1999

Client
Vinzentz art in architecture, Düsseldorf

Design
Claus Koch Corporate Communications, Düsseldorf

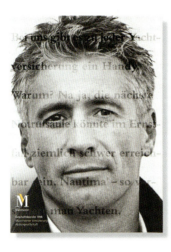

4 Geschäfts-berichte der Mannheimer AG Holding
6/1999
Client Mannheimer Versicherungen, Mannheim
Design Hilger.Boie Büro für Gestaltung, Wiesbaden Clemens Hilger

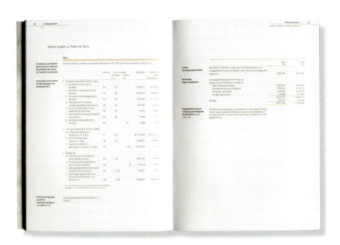

Druckreif	
6/1999	
Client	Bastian Druck, Föhren
Design	Zink & Kraemer, Trier

RADIO CORPORATION
OF SINGAPORE
YEARBOOK 1999

7/1999

CLIENT
Radio Corporation of
Singapore

DESIGN
Epigram PTE LTD,
Singapore
Beh Kay Yi
Paul van der Veer
Edmund Wee

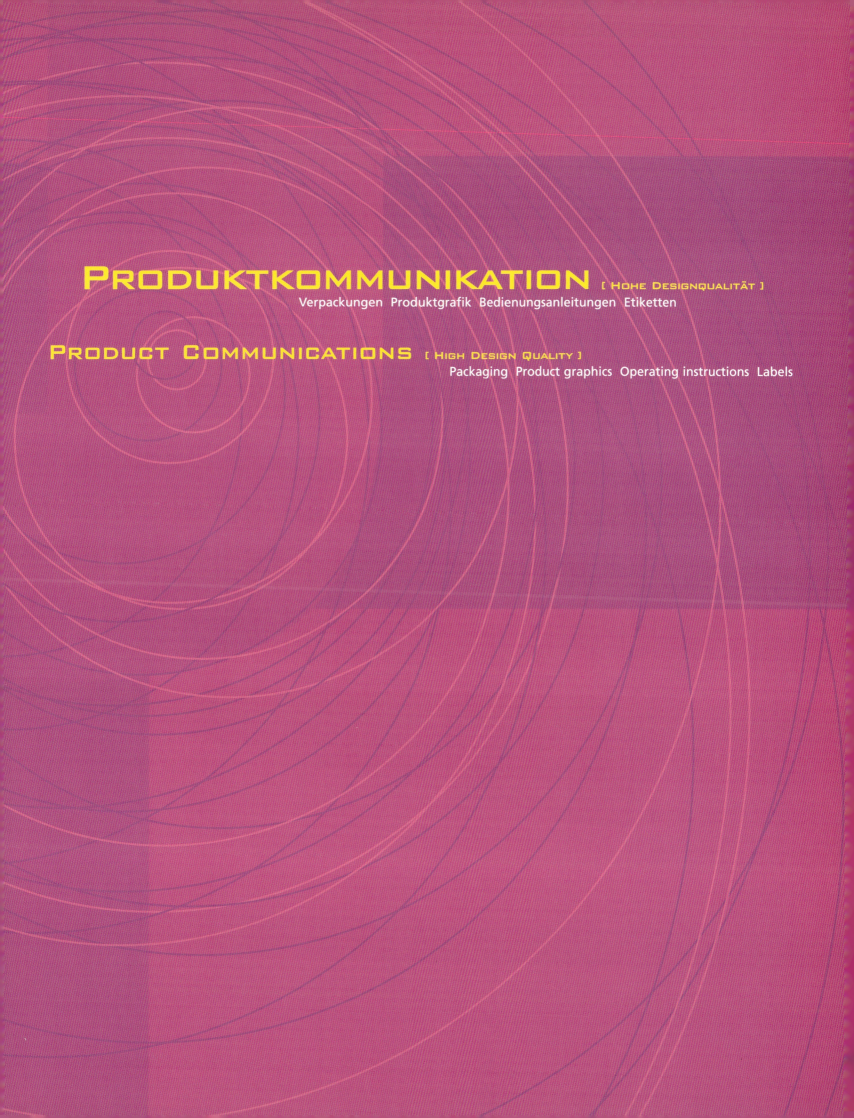

Chinese Tee Xiang Le Selection
2/98
CLIENT
Human Renaissance Corporation, Tokyo, Japan
DESIGN
CID Lab. Inc., Osaka, Japan
Yukichi Takada

Spirit	
1999	
Client	Ruckstuhl AG, Langenthal, Suisse
Design	P'INC. AG, Langenthal, Suisse Urs Hug

Fernsehen und elektronische Medien [Hohe Designqualität]
Sendererscheinungsbilder Programmaufmacher Computergrafiken Trailer Animationen

Television and Electronic Media [High Design Quality]
Broadcasting station images Program lead-ins Computer graphics Trailers Animations

STRANGE WORLD

9/98

CLIENT
Teakwood Lane Productions

DESIGN
Imaginary Forces, Hollywood, USA

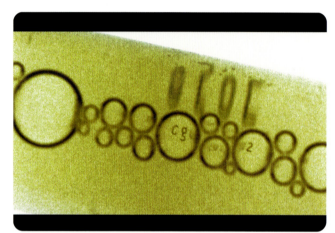
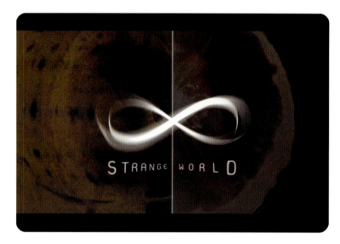
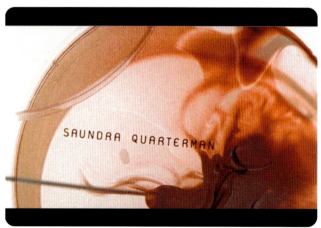

ARLINGTON ROAD

7/99

CLIENT
Polygram
Entertainment
(Mark Pellington),
Beverly Hills, USA

DESIGN
Imaginary Forces,
Hollywood, USA

Dead Man Campus

8/98

Client
MTV Films
(Alan Cohn),
Los Angeles, USA
Paramount,
Los Angeles, USA

Design
Imaginary Forces,
Hollywood, USA

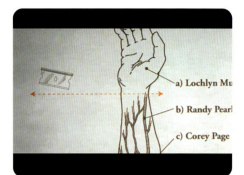
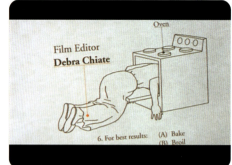

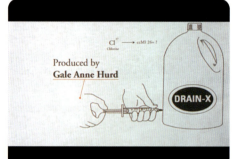
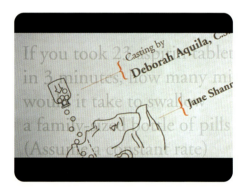
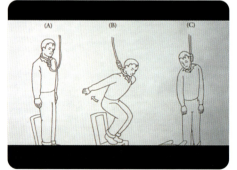
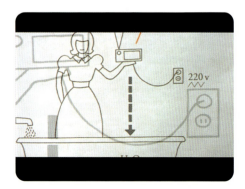

Kultur & Sport [Hohe Designqualität]
Plakate Einladungen Kataloge Veranstaltungserscheinungsbilder Signets Ausstellungen

Culture and sport [High Design Quality]
Posters Invitations Catalogs Images for events Symbols Exhibitions

THE EARTH:
TRIUMPH IN PLASTIC

10/97

CLIENT
UN Framework on
Climate Change in
Kyoto, Japan

DESIGN
Steiner & Co.,
Hong Kong, China
Henry Steiner

Orpheus & Eurydike	
1998	
Client	
Die Clownixen, Simone Fasnacht, Düsseldorf	
Design	
Gesine Grotrian-Steinweg, Düsseldorf Fons M. Hickmann, Düsseldorf	

»Citylights L,S,B«
Nick/Blume/Himmel

5/99

Client
Versorgungs- und
Verkehrsgesellschaft
Saarbrücken,
Saarbrücken

Design
Maksimovic & Partners,
Saarbrücken
AD: Ivica Maksimovic,
Patrick Bittner
Graphics: Isabel Bach
Typography:
Natascha Maksimovic
Photography:
Natascha Maksimovic

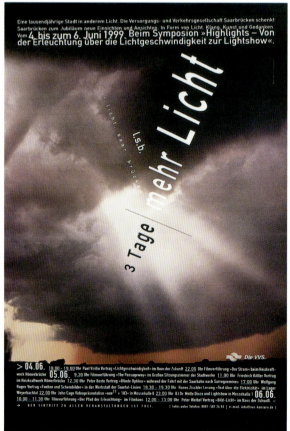

MITTEILUNG »AN-
TRIEBSBOTSCHAFT«
IM GOETHE-JAHR

1/99

DESIGN
botschaft
gertrud nolte
visuelle kommunika-
tion und gestaltung,
Düsseldorf
Gertrud Nolte

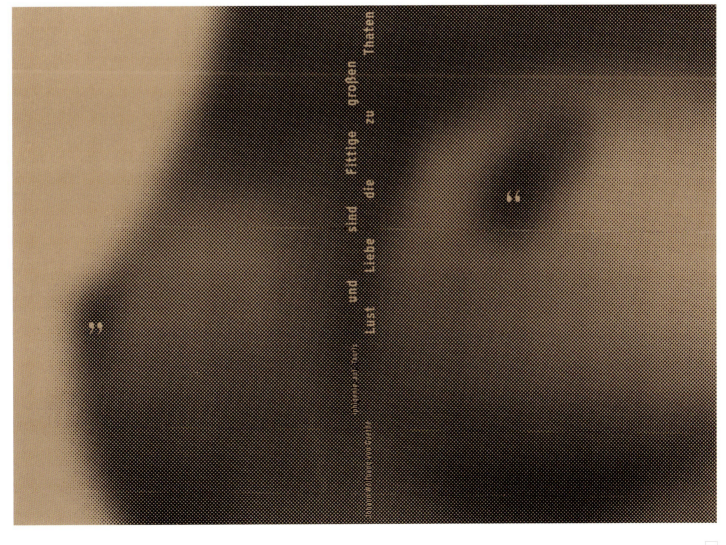

100th Anniversary Kokura technical high school
3/98
Client Kokura technical high school, Fukuoka, Japan
Design Makoto Saito Design Office Inc., Tokyo, Japan Makoto Saito

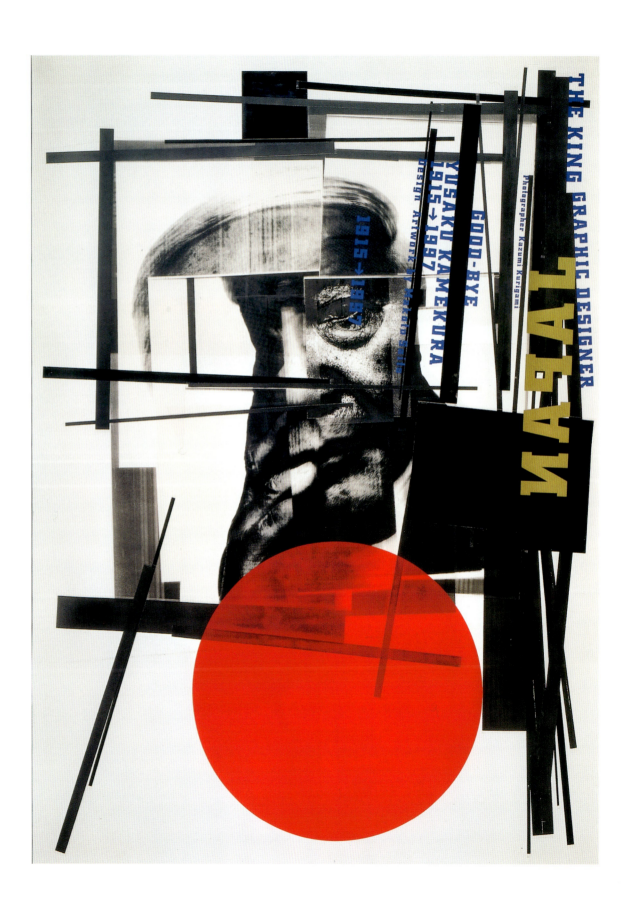

SUNRISE SUNSET
YUSAKA KAMEKURA

4/99

CLIENT
Toppan Printing Co., Ltd.
Makoto Saito Design Office Inc.,
Tokyo, Japan

DESIGN
Makoto Saito Design Office Inc.,
Tokyo, Japan
Makoto Saito

RISING SUN LUNCH IN THE FORM OF THE NATIONAL FLAG OF JAPAN
9/97
CLIENT
Maison de la Culture du Japon à Paris
DESIGN
Makoto Saito Design Office Inc., Tokyo, Japan
Makoto Saito

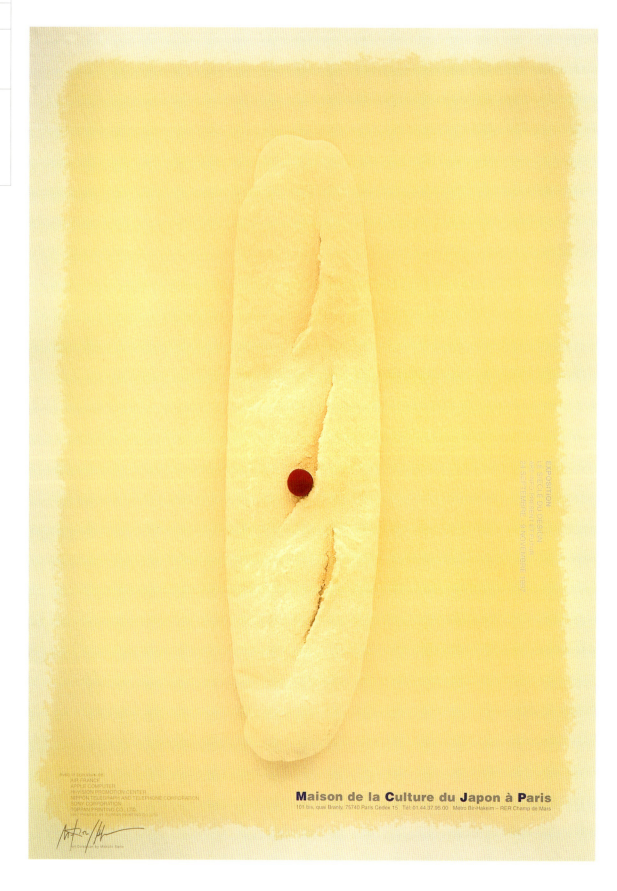

BROSCHÜRE
WENIGER ARBEIT –
ARBEIT FÜR ALLE

4/99

CLIENT
Stadt Wuppertal,
Geschäftsbereich
Soziales und Kultur,
Prof. Uwe Becker

DESIGN
schmitz Agentur für
visuelle Kommunikation, Wuppertal
Thordis Ohler
Hans Günter Schmitz

„Mehr
Zeitsouveränität?
– Chancen
und Risiken
von Arbeitszeit-
verkürzung."

"Shorter working
hours from the
aspect of company
organisation."

CREAM. CONTEMPORARY ART IN CULTURE	
1998	
DESIGN	Phaidon Press, London, Great Britain Julia Hasting

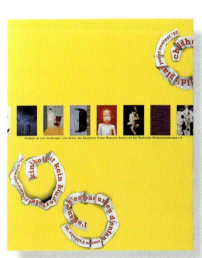

KINDHEIT IST KEIN KINDERSPIEL
1998
CLIENT Deutsches Plakat Museum, Essen
DESIGN verb Agentur für Kommunikations-design GmbH, Essen

Wortbildzeitraum [Juniorpreis]	
8/97	
Client	Fachhochschule Düsseldorf, Fachbereich Design, Düsseldorf
Design	Ralf Weißmantel, Düsseldorf

RETROSPEKTIVE ANGELIKA KAUFFMANN

8/99

CLIENT
Kunstmuseum Düsseldorf
Dr. Bettina Baumgärtel

DESIGN
Grafikbüro, Düsseldorf
Petra Knyrim
Stefan Nowak
Philipp Teufel mit
Anke von Bremen
Nicole Rother
Dominik Mycielsky

Gesina Liebe, Broschüre Reliquien	
1998	
Client	Gesina Liebe, Köln
Design	Rempen Partner: Das Design Büro, Düsseldorf Stefan Baggen

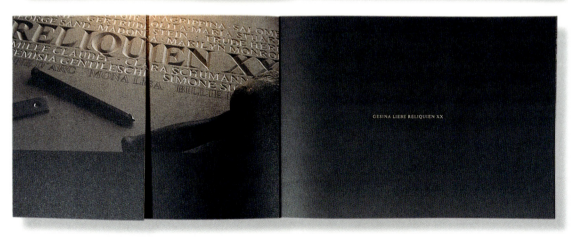

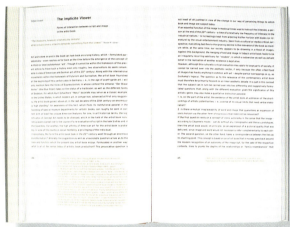

HANK HINE-
KATALOG

1998 / 99

CLIENT
Staatliche Kunsthalle
Karlsruhe
(Kunstmuseum Bonn,
Richter Verlag
Düsseldorf)

DESIGN
Monika Hagenberg,
Meerbusch

VERLAGSWESEN [Hohe Designqualität]
Bücher Zeitschriften Karten CD- und Cassetten-Cover Kalender Illustrationen

PUBLISHING [High Design Quality]
Books Magazines Cards CD and Cassettes Cover Calendars Illustrations

JUBILÄUMSBUCH

1998

CLIENT
RIAS Kammerchor,
Berlin

DESIGN
K/PLEX Konzepte für
Kommunikation
GmbH, Berlin
Dominika Hasse
Grit Neufang

Memorabilia

2/99

Client
Van+Van Publiciteit,
Maarssen,
The Netherlands

Design
UNA (Amsterdam)
designers,
The Netherlands
André Cremer
Hans Bockting

Der Umgang mit
den Dingen
[Juniorpreis]

2/99

Design
Jochen Tratz,
Würzburg

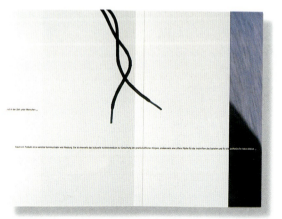
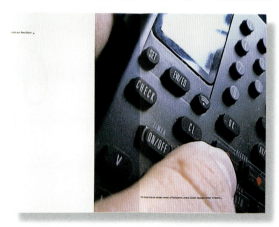

RAUMFAHRT VERSUCH EINER UNMÖGLICHEN RAUMDEFINITION [JUNIORPREIS]
2 / 99
CLIENT Merz Akademie, Prof. Joost Bottema, Stuttgart
DESIGN Marc T. Bernauer, Köln

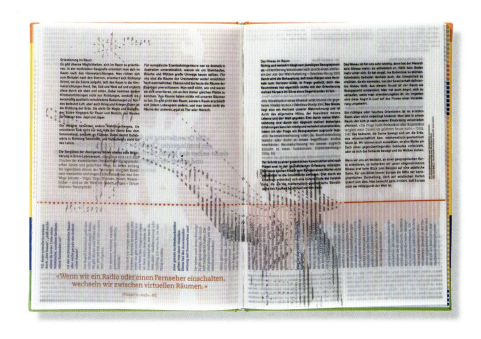

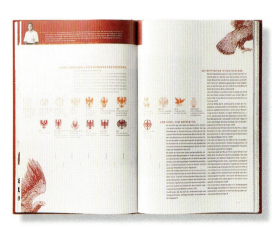

MACHTSPIELE
[JUNIORPREIS]

5/99

CLIENT
Fachhochschule Potsdam
Prof. Dr. Rainer Funke,
Prof. Betina Müller,
Potsdam

DESIGN
Marion Wagner, Berlin

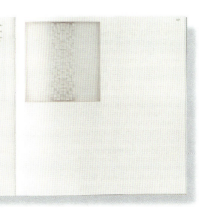

TONSPUR

11/98

CLIENT
Museum für Neue Kunst und Modo Verlag, Freiburg

DESIGN
Grafikbüro, Düsseldorf
Petra Knyrim
Stefan Nowak
Philipp Teufel
mit Dominik Mycielski
Yvonne Günther

ARTUR No 17 EINE FÄLSCHERNUMMER
10/98
CLIENT ARTUR-Forum für Kunst und Kultur, Augsburg
DESIGN LIQIUID Agentur für Gestaltung, Augsburg Ilja Sallacz

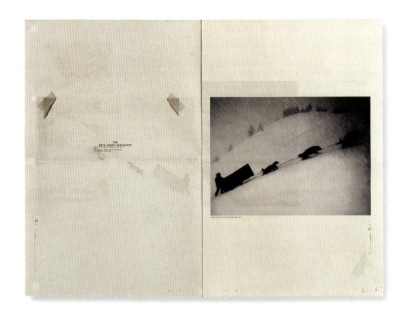

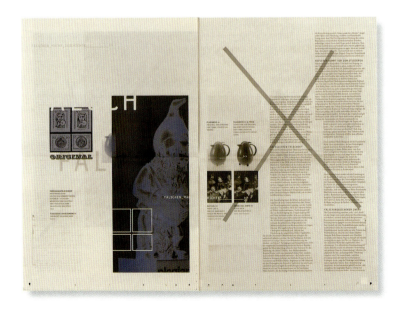

EIN DENKMAL GESETZT

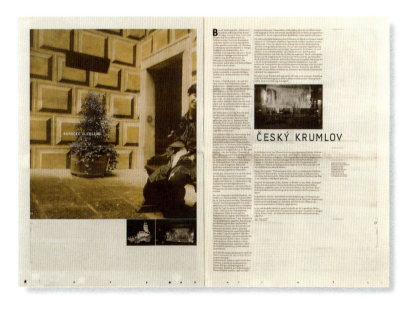

BAROCKE ILLUSION

ČESKÝ KRUMLOV

ZEITUNG »KULTUR«

1997 / 98 / 99

CLIENT
Kulturgemeinschaft, Stuttgart

DESIGN
Kurt Ranger Design, Stuttgart

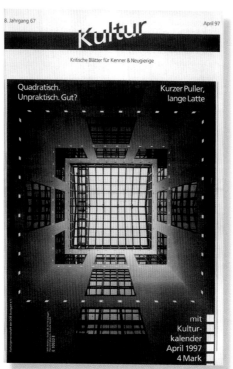

Rund um Berlin	
1998	
Client	
Verlag Haus am Checkpoint Charlie, Berlin	
Design	
Armin Lindauer, Berlin	

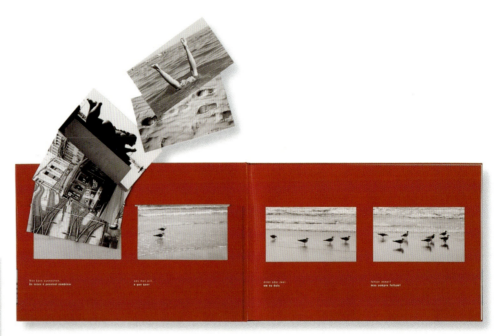

CAMINHOS- VON WEGEN	
1998	
CLIENT	Ruth Gschwendtner, Feldkirch, Austria
DESIGN	Lürzer Graphik, Götzis, Austria Klaus Lürzer

TISCHKALENDER

12/98

CLIENT
Contrapunkt _Visuelle Kommunikation, Tutzing

DESIGN
Patrick Vallee Design, München
Patrick Vallee

PUBLIKATION &
KOMMUNIKATIONS-
MEDIEN ZUM THEMA
SCHWARZ
[JUNIORPREIS]

2/98

DESIGN
Sabrina Lyhs,
Düsseldorf

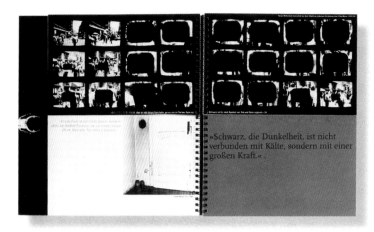

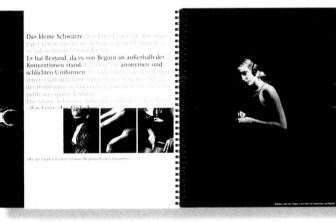

LOOKING BACK FREEMAN LAU'S POSTER DESIGN-BOOK
1999
CLIENT Kan & Lau Design Consultants, Hong Kong, China
DESIGN Kan & Lau Design Consultants, Hong Kong, China Freeman Lau Siu Hong

JAHRESKALENDER
1999
1999
CLIENT
Van der Ven-Dental GmbH & Co. KG, Duisburg
Druckhaus Louisgang GmbH, Gelsenkirchen
DESIGN
vE & K Werbeagentur GmbH & Co. KG, Essen
Tilo Karl
Gaby van Emmerich
Ursula Röttger

6. Edition
12/98
Client
Claus Koch Corporate Communications, Düsseldorf
Design
Claus Koch Corporate Communications, Düsseldorf

SIMPLY EATING
[JUNIORPREIS]
2/99
CLIENT
designkantine, Sandra Baumer, Bremen
DESIGN
Sandra Baumer, Berlin

Eye Magazine
Issues 29, 31, 32
1998/99

Client
Quantum Publishing,
Croydon, Great Britain

Design
UNA (London)
designers,
London, Great Britain
Nick Bell
Sacha Davison

Einblicke – ein schriftgestalterisches Experiment [Juniorpreis]
1999
Design
Andrea Petry, Koblenz

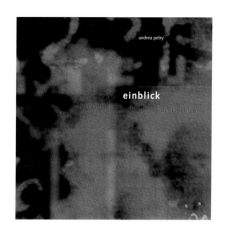

Multimedia [Hohe Designqualität]
CD-ROM/CD-I Online-Gestaltung/Homepages

Multimedia [High Design Quality]
CD-ROM/CD-I Online design/homepages

Die neue S-Klasse. Sinn und Sinnlichkeit
9/98
Client DaimlerChrysler AG, Stuttgart
Design Scholz & Volkmer Intermediales Design GmbH, Wiesbaden

**Bacardi-Website
Get the ritmo de
Bacardi**

6/99

Client
Bacardi GmbH,
Hamburg

Design
Melle.Pufe.Thiessen,
Berlin

WWW.SCHOLZ-UND-VOLKMER.DE

7/99

CLIENT
Scholz & Volkmer
Intermediales Design
GmbH, Wiesbaden

DESIGN
Scholz & Volkmer
Intermediales Design
GmbH, Wiesbaden

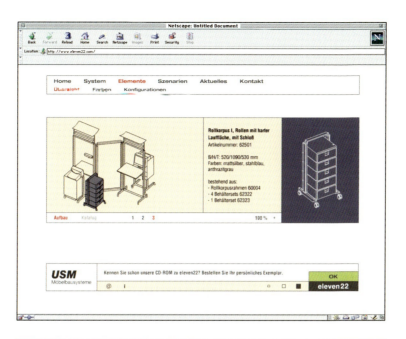

WWW.ELEVEN22.COM

5/99

CLIENT
USM U. Schärer
Söhne AG,
Münsingen, Suisse

DESIGN
Scholz & Volkmer
intermediales Design
GmbH, Wiesbaden

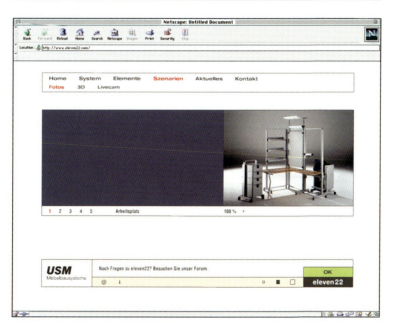

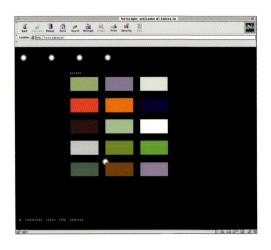

WWW.KAIROS.TO

6/99

CLIENT
escale, Düsseldorf
nonex, Düsseldorf
Gesine Grotrian-
Steinweg, Düsseldorf
Fons M. Hickmann,
Düsseldorf

DESIGN
Gesine Grotrian-
Steinweg, Düsseldorf
Fons M. Hickmann,
Düsseldorf

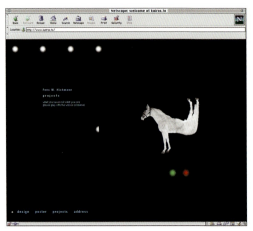

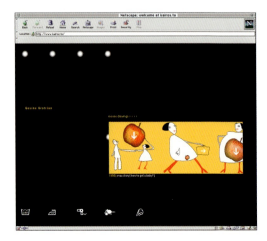

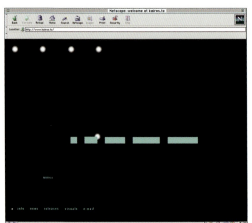

Internetauftritt

12/98

Design
Maksimovic & Partners,
Saarbrücken
AD: Ivica Maksimovic,
Patrick Bittner
Graphics/Photography:
Patrick Bittner
Text: Ono Mothwurf,
Ivica Maksimovic
Production/Screen
Design: Patrick Bittner,
Hendrik Becker

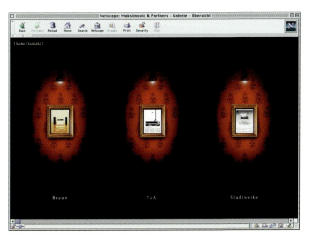

EMBASSY OF DREAMS
WWW.EMBASSY.DE

7/99

CLIENT
Embassy of Dreams
Filmproduktion GmbH,
Helmut Hartl,
München

DESIGN
WYSIWYG Software
Design GmbH,
Düsseldorf
Design:
Dirk Uhlenbrock
Text: Stefan Telegdy

BEGA
WWW.BEGA.DE

5/99

CLIENT
Bega Gantenbrink-
Leuchten GmbH+Co,
Bruno Gantenbrink,
Menden

DESIGN
WYSIWYG Software
Design GmbH,
Düsseldorf
Creative Director:
Alexander Koch
Design: Alexander
Koch, Peter Engels
Text: Michael
Lorscheider
Anett Kryczanowski

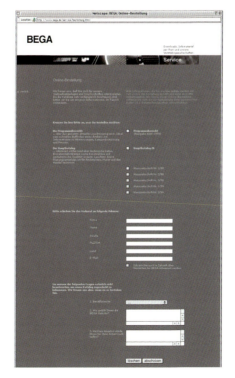

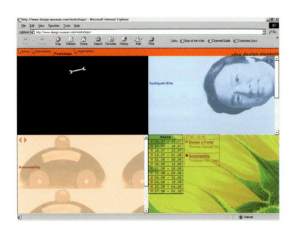

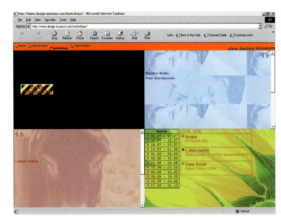

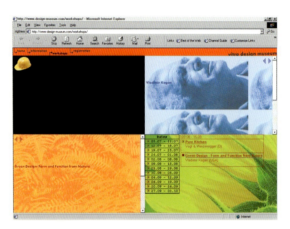

VITRA DESIGN
MUSEUM SUMMER
WORKSHOP
WEBSITE

3/99

CLIENT
Vitra Design Museum,
Weil am Rhein

DESIGN
Virtual Identity,
Freiburg
Kati Kopf
Sonja Schäfer
Uli Weidner

VITRA MARKETING INFORMATIONSSYSTEM

5/99

CLIENT
Vitra Design Museum, Weil am Rhein

DESIGN
Virtual Identity, Freiburg
Sonja Schäfer
Uli Weidner

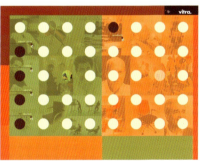
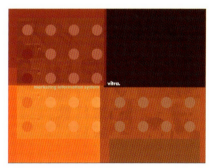
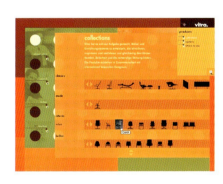

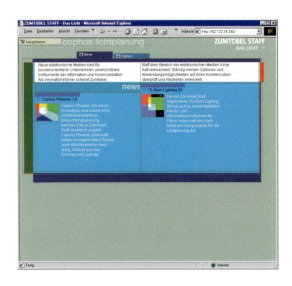

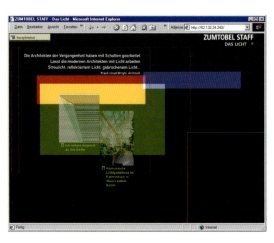

Zumtobel Staff	
Website	
4/99	
Client	
Zumtobel Staff GmbH, Dornbirn, Austria	
Design	
Virtual Identity, Freiburg	
Oliver Habboub	
Uli Weidner	

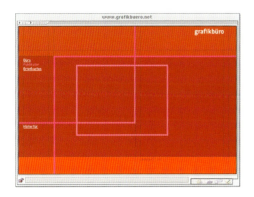

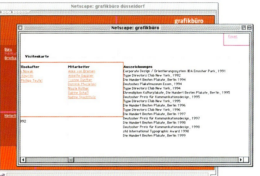

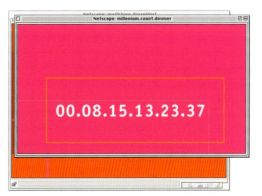

WWW.GRAFIKBÜRO.NET

1998

CLIENT
Grafikbüro, Düsseldorf

DESIGN
Grafikbüro, Düsseldorf
Petra Knyrim
Stefan Novak
Philipp Teufel mit
Dominik Mycielski

GESCHICHTE EINER BANK UND EINER FAMILIE

1/99

CLIENT
Sal. Oppenheim
Jr & Cie., Köln

DESIGN
Foco Media GmbH &
Cie., München
Christian von Sanden

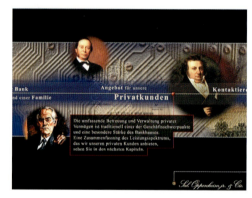

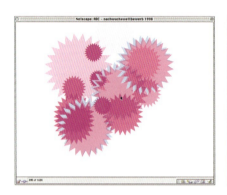
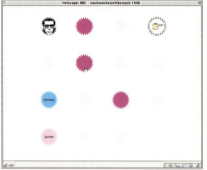

WWW.ADC.DE/SUSHI	
1999	
Client	Art Directors Club für Deutschland e.V., Frankfurt
Design	Hesse Designstudios GmbH, Düsseldorf/ Universität GH Essen Frank Hellenkamp Klaus Hesse Stefan Landrock Lars Loick

WWW.O-TEL-O.DE

1/98

CLIENT
Mannesmann o.tel.o
GmbH, Düsseldorf

DESIGN
KABEL NEW MEDIA
GmbH, Hamburg

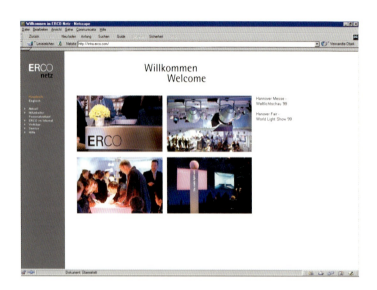
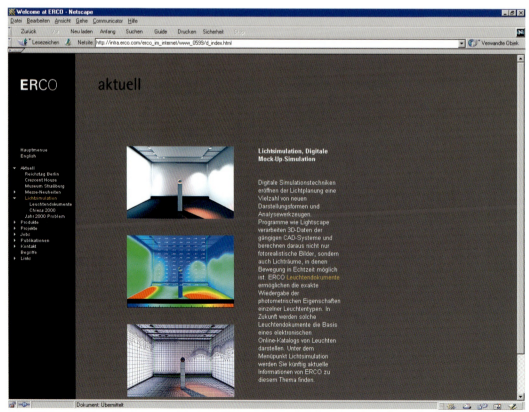

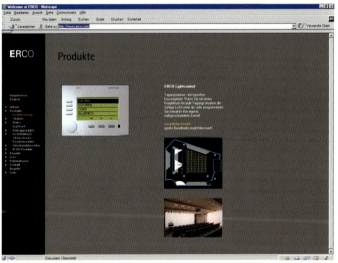

WWW.ERCO.COM

6/99

CLIENT
ERCO Leuchten GmbH, Lüdenscheid

DESIGN
Visuelle Kommunikation Monika Schnell, Neu-Ulm / Wekemann + Schöls GmbH, Stuttgart

Die Form der Kommunikation?

Peter Zec

Heute kommt es darauf an, die Form der Kommunikation in der Wirtschaft prinzipiell in Frage zu stellen. Noch nie zuvor wurde so viel Geld für Werbung ausgegeben wie dies heute geschieht. Andererseits scheint im Gegenzug dazu die Wirkungskraft der Werbung überproportional stark abzunehmen. Dennoch - oder besser gesagt - gerade deshalb, wird noch mehr in die Werbung investiert. Als ein Argument der Rechtfertigung für dieses paradoxe Verhalten mag gelten, daß niemand so recht wissen kann, was geschähe, wenn man statt mehr, weniger oder sogar nichts mehr in die Werbung investieren würde.

Soweit wollen viele Marketingdirektoren erst gar nicht denken. Statt dessen machen sie lieber weiter wie bisher. Wenn es dann trotzdem Probleme mit dem Umsatz gibt, wird allenfalls die Werbeagentur, nicht aber die Werbung an sich in Frage gestellt. Werbung muß eben sein, ganz gleich von wem sie gemacht wird. Die Werbemacher werden immer austauschbarer, weil Werbung offensichtlich mehr und mehr zum Selbstzweck wird. Wichtig ist, daß sie geschieht, nicht warum und wozu dies erforderlich ist. So erklärt sich auch die zunehmende Auftragsfluktuation in der Werbewelt. Werbeetats werden in der Branche bisweilen fast ähnlich gehandelt wie Aktienpakete. Gefragt sind neue, »kreative« Ideen und Konzepte. Die Form der Kommunikation jedoch wird dabei prinzipiell nicht in Frage gestellt. Sie ist in der Werbung bis heute immer gleich geblieben. Ganz gleich mit welchem Medium Werbung geschieht, ob als Plakat, Anzeige oder TV-Spot, stets ist die Form der Kommunikation dabei durch Linearität und Iteration geprägt. Als Form betrachtet handelt es sich bei der Werbung um die ständige Wiederkehr des Immergleichen, ganz unabhängig davon, was inhaltlich eigentlich beabsichtigt ist.

Es ist die Form der Kommunikation, die dazu führt, daß Werbung heute von immer mehr Menschen als bloßer Selbstzweck oder als eine ästhetische Form an sich wahrgenommen wird.

Michael Schirner hat dies ja schon vor langer Zeit erkannt und mit seiner Feststellung »Werbung ist Kunst« zum Ausdruck gebracht. Inzwischen kann man die Aussage noch weiter konkretisieren: Werbung ist l'art pour l'art. Eine Kunst der Kunst halber. Ästhetizismus pur also. Die Gestaltung der Werbung geschieht im Dienste der Selbstinszenierung, wobei das eigentlich zu bewerbende Unternehmen oder Produkt einen zwar austauschbaren aber dennoch willkommenen Anlaß für das Werbespektakel darstellen. Für ein funktions- und gebrauchsorientiertes Design ist dabei kein Platz.

Die lineare Form der Kommunikation in der Werbung basiert auf der Kausalitätsidee, bei der es um die Verbindung von einer Ursache mit einer Wirkung geht. Der Kommunikationsprozeß wird hierbei auf einen relativ trivialen Mechanismus reduziert. Selbst wenn moderne Marketingdirektoren und Werbemacher es heute vehement bestreiten, daß sich ihr Denken und Handeln nach wie vor an der AIDA-Formel (Attention, Interest, Desire, Action) orientiert, ist de facto eigentlich doch alles beim Alten geblieben. Noch immer soll durch Werbung ein kausaler, linearer Prozess von der Aufmerksamkeit über das Interesse und den Wunsch zum schließlichen Kauf in Gang gesetzt werden. Damit Werbung dies leisten kann, müßte jedoch die Transformationsregel zwischen Ursache und Wirkung bekannt sein. Man müßte also wissen, welche Art der Aussage zu der gewünschten Kaufhandlung beim Adressaten führt.

Früher hat es mal Menschen gegeben, die fest an die Bestimmbarkeit dieses Prozesses zum Zwecke der Handlungsmanipulation geglaubt haben. Heute jedoch können wir mit großer Gewißheit davon ausgehen, daß niemand über dieses Wissen verfügt, weil es prinzipiell unmöglich ist, dieses Wissen zu haben. Deshalb basiert Werbung noch immer auf dem Prinzip eines trial and error-Verfahrens und nicht auf einem rationalen Kalkül. So kann man auch verstehen, warum immer mehr Unternehmen es immer öfter mit anderen Werbeagenturen versuchen, erfolgreich zu sein. Solange dabei jedoch die Form der linearen Kommunikation mit Werbung nicht in Frage gestellt wird, wird sich auch an diesem Prozedere zwischen Unternehmen und Werbeagenturen nichts ändern. Hier stellt sich wiederum die Frage, wieviele Unternehmen es sich wohl noch wie lange leisten können, diese Form der Kommunikation nicht in Frage zu stellen?

The Form of Communication?

Peter Zec

Today it is important to principally question the form of communication in the economy. Never before has so much money been spent on advertising. On the other hand, it appears that on the contrary the effect of advertising has disproportionately decreased. Nevertheless, or rather precisely for this reason, more and more is being invested in advertising. An argument to justify this paradoxical behaviour is that no-one can really know what would happen if less or even nothing were invested in advertising rather than more.

Many marketing directors do not even want to think that far ahead. Instead, they would rather continue as before. If there are still problems with turnover then it is always the agency and not the advertising itself, which is questioned. Advertising is necessary – irrespective of who does it. Advertisers are becoming increasingly replaceable as advertising has obviously become more of an end to itself. What is important is that it exists, not the reason or purpose behind it.

This explains the increasing amount of fluctuating jobs in the world of advertising. Now and then advertising budgets in the field are dealt in a similar way to share packages. New »creative« ideas and concepts are demanded. The form of communication is however not principally questioned here. As yet it has remained the same in advertising.

Regardless of which medium the advertising uses whether it is posters, adverts, or TV commercials, the form of communication is constantly characterised by linearity and interaction. Considered as a form, advertising always deals with the continual recurrence of the same thing, completely independent of what is actually intended.

It is the form of communication that leads to the fact that advertising today is perceived by more and more people as merely an end in itself or as an aesthetic form.

Michael Schirner recognised this a long time ago expressing it with the statement »Advertising is Art«. In the meantime the statement can be made more concrete: Advertising is l'art pour l'art. Art for art's sake. Pure aestheticism. The creation of advertising is done for its own sake whereby the company or product that is to actually be advertised may be replaceable but still be a welcome opportunity to present an advertising spectacle. There is no room for functional and consumer-oriented design.

The linear form of communication in advertising is based on the idea of causality, which deals with the correlation between cause and effect. Here the communication process is reduced to a relatively trivial mechanism. Even when modern marketing directors and advertisers argue vehemently that their thinking and actions are, as always, oriented towards the AIDA formula (Attention, Interest, Desire, Action), in actual fact it has stayed the same. Even now there should still be a causal linear process: attention, interest, and subsequently the desire to buy should be set into motion. So that advertising can afford to do this, the transformation rules between cause and effect should be known. One should also know which type of statement leads to the desired action of buying by those addressed.

Previously there were people who firmly believed in the determinability of these processes to manipulate actions. Today, however, we can justifiably assume that no one has this knowledge as it is principally impossible to have. Therefore advertising is based on the principle of trial and error and not on rational calculations. For this reason one can understand why more and more companies try their luck with different advertising agencies with increased frequency. So long, however, as the form of linear communication with advertising is not questioned. And as long as this happens the procedures between companies and advertising agencies will not change. Here, on the other hand, it has to be asked how many companies can continue to be able to afford to not question this form of communication.

Anhang
Jury Gestalter Auftraggeber

Appendix
Jury Designer Clients

JURY

Hans P. Brandt
studierte Grafik-Design und Kommunikationswissenschaften an der Hochschule der Künste Berlin. Er hat an zahlreichen Hochschulen und Instituten unterrichtet, u.a. an der Kunstgewerbeschule Zürich, der Hochschule der Künste Berlin und dem Internationalen Design Zentrum Berlin. Seit 1988 ist er bei Total Design in Amsterdam tätig, seit 1996 in der Funktion eines Direktors, seit 1997 auch als Partner.

Hans P. Brandt
studied graphic design and communication sciences at the University of Fine Arts in Berlin. He has taught at numerous universities and institutes e.g. School for Arts and Crafts in Zurich, University of Fine Arts in Berlin and at the International Design Center in Berlin. Since 1988 he has been working with Total Design in Amsterdam, where he became director in 1996 and partner in 1997.

Christof Gassner
studierte an der Kunstgewerbeschule Zürich. Nach Tätigkeiten in Industrie und Verlag (»Öko-Test Magazin«, »natur«), gründete er ein eigenes Grafik-Design-Atelier in Frankfurt am Main, seit 1992 lebt und arbeitet er in Darmstadt. Er ist Mitglied in der AGI Alliance Graphique Internationale, Dozent für Grafik-Design und Typographie an der Universität Gesamthochschule Kassel.

Christof Gassner
studied at the Arts and Crafts School in Zurich. After working in industry and publishing (»Öko-Test Magazin«, »natur«), he founded his own graphic design atelier in Frankfurt am Main. He has been living and working in Darmstadt since 1992. He is a member of the AGI Alliance Graphique Internationale, lecturer in graphic design and typography at the Comprehensive University in Kassel.

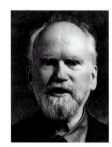

Günter Gerhard Lange
studierte an der Staatlichen Akademie für grafische Künste und Buchgewerbe in Leipzig und an der Hochschule für Bildende Künste in Berlin. Von 1952-1960 war er Dozent für typographische Gestaltung an der Meisterschule für Graphik, Druck und Werbung in Berlin, ab 1959 künstlerischer Leiter der H. Berthold AG Berlin/München. Er hat Lehraufträge an der Fachschule für Industriewerbung und Absatzförderung in Kassel, der Kunstschule Alsterdamm in Hamburg sowie der Werbefachlichen Akademie in München wahrgenommen. Seit 1974 ist er Dozent für Visuelle Kommunikation am Lehrinstitut für graphische Gestaltung in München U5 und seit 1997 an der Hochschule für angewandte Kunst in Wien.

Günter Gerhard Lange
studied at the State Academy for Graphic Arts and Print Industry in Leipzig and the University of Fine Arts in Berlin. From 1952 to 1960 he was a lecturer in typographic design at the Master School for Graphics, Printing and Advertising in Berlin; since 1959 he has been working as art director at H. Berthold Inc., Berlin/Munich. He accepted special teaching posts at the School of Industrial Advertising and Sales Promotion in Kassel, the Alsterdamm School of Art in Hamburg and the Advertising Academy in Munich U5. Since 1974 he has been lecturing in visual communication at the Institute for Graphic Design, Munich. Since 1997 he has been a lecturer in typography at the Vienna University for Applied Arts.

Uwe Loesch
Studium und Studio in Düsseldorf, Mitglied der AGI Alliance Graphic Internationale und des ADC Art Directors Club für Deutschland, Professor für Kommunikationsdesign an der Bergischen Universität Wuppertal. Internationale Anerkennung insbesondere in den Bereichen Plakatgestaltung, Corporate Design und Corporate Culture. Zahlreiche Preise und Auszeichnungen, Einzel- und Gruppenausstellungen, Buchveröffentlichungen und Publikationen seiner Arbeiten - weltweit. Seit 1983 mit mehreren Arbeiten im Museum of Modern Art, New York, 1995 Grand Prix des Deutschen Preises für Kommunikationsdesign.

Uwe Loesch
studied and has a studio in Düsseldorf, member of the AGI, Alliance Graphique Internationale and ADC Art Directors Club for Germany, professor of communication design at Bergische Universität Wuppertal. International acclaim especially in the fields of poster design, corporate design and corporate culture. Numerous awards and prizes, solo and group shows, book publications and publications of his works - worldwide. Since 1983 several of his works have been on display in the Museum of Modern Art, New York. In 1995 he was awarded the German Prize for Communication Design.

Kurt Weidemann

absolvierte eine Schriftsetzerlehre in Lübeck, studierte an der Staatlichen Akademie der Bildenden Künste in Stuttgart und arbeitete als Schriftleiter beim »Druckspiegel«. Heute arbeitet der Designer, Typograph und Texter neben seiner umfangreichen Lehrtätigkeit (Stuttgart, Karlsruhe, Koblenz) als Berater großer Unternehmen. So konzipierte er für den Daimler-Benz-Konzern das Erscheinungsbild und die Design-Richtlinien. Auch die Erscheinungsbilder der Firmen Coop, Merck und Zeiss sowie das der Deutschen Bahn AG wurden von ihm entwickelt. 1995 wurde er mit dem Lucky Strike Designer Award, Europas höchst dotiertem Designer-Preis und dem Verdienstorden 1. Klasse der Bundesrepublik geehrt.

Kurt Weidemann

served as an apprenticeship typesetter in Lübeck before attending the State Academy of Arts in Stuttgart. He then became editor of »Der Druckspiegel« . The designer, typographer and copywriter, aside from his extensive pedagogical endeavours (Stuttgart, Karlsruhe, Koblenz), works as a consultant for large enterprises. For Daimler-Benz, for example, he established the corporate design and design guidelines. He also developed the public image of Coop, Merck and Zeiss as well as Deutsche Bahn AG. In 1995 he was honoured with the Lucky Strike Designer Award, the most highly regarded design award in Europe and with Verdienstorden 1. Klasse of the Federal Republic of Germany.

Jutta Nachtwey

studierte Illustration und Kommunikationsdesign an der Fachhochschule für Gestaltung in Hamburg, danach Kunstgeschichte, Germanistik und Spanisch an der Universität Hamburg. Seit 1994 arbeitet sie für die Redaktion der Zeitschrift PAGE, zuletzt als Leitende Redakteurin, heute freiberuflich als Fachjournalistin. Daneben wirkt sie bei Publikationen als Redakteurin und Herausgeberin mit.

Jutta Nachtwey

studied illustration and communication design at the College for Design in Hamburg and following this she studied art history, German studies and Spanish at the University of Hamburg. Since 1994 she has been working on the editorial staff of the magazine PAGE, in the end as leading editor. Today she works as a trade journalist and in addition to this, she works as editor and publisher on various publications.

Iris Utikal

studierte Visuelle Kommunikation an der Fachhochschule Düsseldorf. Nach dem Diplom arbeitete sie in der Arbeitsgemeinschaft Loesch und gründete 1994 zusammen mit Michael Gais das Büro QWER, seit 1995 mit Sitz in Köln. Arbeitsschwerpunkte sind im Bereich des Corporate Designs und der Ausstellungskommunikation. QWER entwarf und betreut unter anderem das Erscheinungsbild der Weltausstellung EXPO 2000 Hannover.

Iris Utikal

studied visual communication at the Düsseldorf College. Following his degree he worked in the working cooperative Loesch and founded the QWER Offices with Michael Gais in 1994. The offices have been located in Cologne since 1995. Her focus lies in the areas of corporate design and exhibition communication. Amongst others, QWER has designed and supervised the appearance of the World Exhibition, EXPO 2000 in Hanover.

Jean Widmer

studierte an der Kunstgewerbeschule Zürich, dann an der Ecole des Beaux-Arts in Paris. Er arbeitete als Art Director der Werbeagentur SNIP, der Galeries Lafayette und der Modezeitschrift »Jardin des Modes«. Seit 1969 entwirft er Erscheinungsbilder und Leitsysteme, Touristeninformationssysteme für Autobahnen sowie Ausstellungsgrafik und Plakate für Museen. 1991 wurde er zum »Officier de l'ordre des Art et des Lettres« ernannt, 1994 erhielt er den großen Nationalpreis der grafischen Kunst (vom Kulturministerium).

Jean Widmer

studied at the Art and Crafts School in Zurich and then at the Ecole des Beaux-Arts in Paris. He worked as art director at the advertising agency SNIP, the Galeries Lafayette and the fashion magazine »Jardin des Modes«. Since 1969 he has been designing appearances, signage systems and tourist information systems for motorways as well as exhibition graphics and posters for museums. In 1991 he was named »Officier de l'ordre des Art et des Lettres« and in 1994 he received the renowned national prize in graphic art (from the Ministry of Arts).

GESTALTER
DESIGNER

Aperto Multimedia
Novalisstraße 11
D-10115 Berlin

ArGe Multimedia GmbH
Boisseréestraße 3
D-50674 Köln

Artes de México
Plaza Río de Janeiro 52
Colonia Roma
México D.F. 06700

Atelier Beinert & Sonner
Kaulbachstraße 92
D-80802 München
34, 39

Sandra Baumer
Thrasoltstraße 7-9
D-10585 Berlin

Beithan, Heßler
Werbeagentur GmbH
Cronstettenstraße 64
D-60322 Frankfurt
102

BEK
Bülent Erkmen
Cihangir Cadessi 18
TR-80060, Istanbul

Marc T. Bernauer
Görrestr. 7
D-50674 Köln
153

Bertelsmann AG
Carl-Bertelsmann-Straße 270
D-33311 Gütersloh
82, 83

Bilek & Co
Werbeagentur GWA
Tübinger Straße 16
D-70187 Stuttgart
92, 93

BOROS GmbH
Hofaue 63
D-42103 Wuppertal
66

botschaft gertrud nolte
visuelle kommunikation und
gestaltung
merowingerstraße 5
D-40233 düsseldorf
135

Brasilhaus No.8 GmbH
Am Wall 175-177
D-28195 Bremen
112, 113

Tina Bühling
Krampasplatz 4c
D-14199 Berlin
30, 31

Büro Hamburg
Hohe Brücke 1
D-20459 Hamburg
101

Eric van Casteren
ontwerpers
Wassenaarseweg 7
NL-2596 CD Den Haag
110, 111

CID Lab. Inc.
2-4-3-603 Uchihommachi
Chuo-ku Osaka 540-0026,
Japan
122

df Type,
Karner & Stefan OEG
Grossmaierhof 15
A-3242 Texing
75

designkantine
Sandra Baumer
Thrasoltstraße 7-9
D-10585 Berlin
167

Eclat, AG für Corporate
Identity
und Mediengestaltung
Seestraße 78
CH-8703 Erlenbach

Epigram PTE LTD
100 Beach Road
#22-04/05 Shaw Towers
Singapore 189702
118

Factor Design AG
Schulterblatt 58
D-20357 Hamburg
35, 36, 99

Fleischmann & Kirsch
Studio für visuelle und
verbale Kommunikation
Landhausstraße 28
D-70190 Stuttgart
65, 104, 105

Foco Media GmbH & Cie.
Spitzwegstraße 6
D-81373 München
184, 185

FÜSSER_SCHMIDT.
Thomas Füsser, Geli Schmidt
Martensweg 1
D-22083 Hamburg
86

Gerk und Krauss
Konzeptionelle Werbung
Am Alten Stadtpark 9A
D-44791 Bochum
114

Grafikbüro
Lichtstraße 52
D-40235 Düsseldorf
145, 155, 183

Gesine Grotrian-Steinweg
Parkstraße 14
D-40477 Düsseldorf
133, 176

Monika Hagenberg
Mataréstraße 1
D-40667 Meerbusch
147

Hebe Werbung & Design
Magstadter Straße 12
D-71229 Leonberg
90, 91

Hesse Designstudios GmbH
Rosmarinstraße 12k
D-40235 Düsseldorf
186

Fons M. Hickmann
Parkstraße 14
D-40477 Düsseldorf
133, 176

Hilger.Boie
Büro für Gestaltung
Geisbergstraße 1
D-65193 Wiesbaden
116

Peter Horlacher
Büro für Gestaltung
Gutenbergstraße 94a
70197 Stuttgart
88

im stall gmbh
agentur für marken- und
medienkonzepte
kastanienallee 84
D-10435 berlin
106, 107

Imaginary Forces
6526 Sunset Blvd
Hollywood CA 90028, USA
54, 74, 126, 127, 128

in(corporate
Ostertorsteinweg 70/71
D-28203 Bremen
84, 85

INTRO Marketing
Hirsauer Straße 143
D-75180 Pforzheim
98

JvM an der Isar
Schwere-Reiter-Straße 35
D-80797 München
69, 70, 71

Jaray·Visual Concepts
Klosbachstraße 85
CH-8030 Zürich
100

KABEL NEW MEDIA GmbH
Schulterblatt 58
D-20357 Hamburg
187

K/PLEX Konzepte für
Kommunikation GmbH
Köpenicker Str.aße 48/49
D-10179 Berlin
150

Kan & Lau Design
Consultants
28/F Great Smart Tower
230 Wanchai Road
Hong Kong
164

Guido Kasper
Gestaltung AGD
Moorstr. 2
D-78467 Konstanz
97

Katsui Design Office, Inc.
3-48-9 Nishihara, Shibuya-ku
Tokyo 151-0066, Japan

KMS
Anzingerstraße 3
D-81671 München
103

Claus Koch
Corporate Communications
Kaistraße 18
D-40211 Düsseldorf
115, 166

Lutz Krause
Gestaltung AGD
Hafenstraße 10
D-78462 Konstanz
97

Külling + Partner Identity
Mühlebachstraße 20
CH-8008 Zürich
96

Oliver Leichsenring
Parkstraße 7
D-06618 Naumburg
68

**Burkhardt Leitner
constructiv GmbH & Co.**
Am Bismarckturm 39
D-70192 Stuttgart
55, 104, 105

**Leonhardt & Kern
Werbung GmbH**
Olgastraße 80
D-70182 Stuttgart
42, 43, 62, 63

Limage Dangereuse
Pelgrimsstraat 3
NL-3029 BH Rotterdam
18, 19, 20, 21

Armin Lindauer
Philippistraße 10
D-14059 Berlin
159

**LIQUID
Agentur für Gestaltung**
Bahnhofstraße 10 RGB
D-86150 Augsburg
156, 157

**Loermann & Schrödter
Werbeagentur GmbH**
Brandstorstraße 9
D-45239 Essen
78

Büro Longjaloux GmbH
Warndtstraße 7
D-42285 Wuppertal
59

Lürzer Graphik
Neuburgstraße 4c
A-6840 Götzis
160

Sabrina Lyhs
Visuelle Kommunikation
Jahnstraße 28
D-40215 Düsseldorf
162, 163

m/w design
149 Wooster Street
NY 10012 New York, USA

**Makoto Saito
Design Office Inc.**
2-27-14 Jingumae Shibuya-ku
Tokyo 150-0001, Japan
136, 137, 138, 139, 140

Maksimovic & Partners
Johannisstraße 5
D-66111 Saarbrücken
94, 134, 177

Melle.Pufe.Thiessen
Münzstraße 15
D-10178 Berlin
173

Metaform bv
Grasweg 57
NL-1031 HX Amsterdam

Hermann Michels
Pickartsberg 6
D-42329 Wuppertal
37

**Hubert Minsch
Kommunikationsdesign**
Robert-Bosch-Straße 11
D-73550 Waldstetten
77

Tamara Narolski
Grandstraße 23
D-45357 Essen
22, 23, 24, 25

Michael·Nash Associates
42-44 Newman Street
GB -London WIP 3PA
76

Neue Digitale
Kaiserstraße 79
D-60329 Frankfurt
33

Nippon Design Center, Inc.
1-13-13, Ginza, Chou-ku
Tokyo 104-0061, Japan
44, 45

Ogilvy & Mather Frankfurt
Hainer Weg 44
D-60599 Frankfurt
28, 60, 109

P`INC. AG
Mühlenweg 14
CH-4900 Langenthal
61, 123

Andrea Petry
Auf der Luh 19
D-56076 Koblenz
169

Polka Design
Steegstraat 12
NL-6041 EA Roermond
38

Atelier Roger Pfund
Communication Visuelle SA
43 Rue Vautier
CH-1227 Carouge (Genève)
29, 52

Phaidon Press
Regents Wharf
All Saints Street
GB-London NI 9PA
142

Proforma Graphic Designers
& Consultants
Sint Jobsweg 30
NL-3024 EJ Rotterdam
48

Kurt Ranger Design
Stuttgarter Straße 77
D-70469 Stuttgart
158

Rempen & Partner:
Das Design Büro
Neuer Zollhof 2
D-40221 Düsseldorf
49, 146

Almut Riebe
Jahnstraße 19
D-60318 Frankfurt
50, 51

Samenwerkende
Ontwerpers
Heerengracht 160
NL-1016 BN Amsterdam
89, 95

Koichi Sato Design Studio
1-35-28-504 Hongo, Bunkyoku
Tokyo 113-0033, Japan

Peter Schmidt Studios
GmbH
Feldbrunnenstaße 27
D-20148 Hamburg
40, 41

schmitz Agentur für
visuelle Kommunikation
Viktoriastraße 87
D-42115 Wuppertal
141

Scholz & Volkmer
Intermediales Design GmbH
Schwalbacher Straße 76
D-65183 Wiesbaden
32, 172, 174, 175

Shape bv
Entrepotdok 72a
NL-1018 AD Amsterdam
108

Steiner & Co.
28c Conduit Road
Hong Kong, China
132

Christian Tönsmann
Grädener Straße 9
D-20257 Hamburg
47

Jochen Tratz
Friedrich-Spee-Straße 27
D-97072 Würzburg
152

Büro Uebele
Visuelle Kommunikation
Paulusstraße 18
D-70197 Stuttgart
64, 67

UNA (Amsterdam) designers
Mauritskade 55
NL-1092 AD Amsterdam
151

UNA (London) designers
5.5 Alaska
500 Building, Grange Road
GB-London SE1 3BA
168

Patrick Vallee Design
Dollmannstraße 17
D-81541 München
161

vE & K Werbeagentur
GmbH & Co. KG
Kortumstraße 45
D-45130 Essen
165

verb Agentur für
Kommunikationsdesign
GmbH
Gelsenkirchener Straße 181
D-45309 Essen
46, 143

Emery Vincent Design
80 Market Street, Southbank
Victoria 3006, Australia
72, 73

Virtual Identity
Gerberau 5
D-79098 Freiburg
180, 181, 182

Visuelle Kommunikation
Monika Schnell
Alte Wiblinger Str. 21
D-89231 Neu-Ulm
188, 189

Marion Wagner
Grunewaldstraße 89
D-10823 Berlin
154

Ralf Weißmantel
Kirchfeldstraße 105
D-40215 Düsseldorf
144

Wekemann + Schöls GmbH
Kommunikation
Alexanderstraße 92
D-70182 Stuttgart
188, 189

Anja Wesner
Grafikdesign
Schneckenburgerstraße 15
D-81675 München
53

WYSIWYG Software Design
GmbH
Neuer Zollhof 2
D-40221 Düsseldorf
178, 179

Zacharko Design
Partnership
208-111 Water Street
Vancouver V6B 1A7
Canada

Zink & Kraemer
Liebfrauenstraße 9
D-54290 Trier
117

AUFTRAGGEBER
CLIENTS

Akademie Bildsprache
Hohe Brücke 1
D-20459 Hamburg
101

Amsterdam RAI
Europaplein
P.O.Box 77777
NL-1078 GZ Amsterdam
108

Apitzsch Proof GmbH
Neumann-Reichardt-Straße
27-33 HS 11
22041 Hamburg
87

Apollo Optik
GmbH & Co. KG
Wallenrodstraße 3
D-91126 Schwabach
69

**Arbeitskreis
Prägefoliendruck e.V.**
Rigistraße 20
D-73037 Göppingen
77

**Art Directors Club für
Deutschland e.V.**
Mellemstraße 22
D-60322 Frankfurt
186

**ARTUR-Forum für Kunst
und Kultur**
Bahnhofsstraße 10 RGB
D-86150 Augsburg
156, 157

Barcardi GmbH
Spitalerstraße 16
D-20095 Hamburg
173

Bastian Druck
Robert-Schuman-Straße 1
D-54343 Föhren
117

**Bat Shalom & Jerusalem
Center for Women**
43 Emek Refaim St.
POB 8083
IL-Jerusalem 91080

**Bauhütte Zeche Zollverein
Schacht XII GmbH**
Gelsenkirchener Straße 181
D-45309 Essen
46

**BEGA Gantenbrink-Leuchten
GmbH + Co.**
Postfach 31 60
58689 Menden
179

Atelier Beinert & Sonner
Kaulbachstr. 92
D-80802 München
34, 39

Berliner Ensemble GmbHG
Bertold-Brecht Platz 1
D-10117 Berlin

Bertelsmann AG
Carl-Bertelsmann-Straße 270
D-33311 Gütersloh
82, 83

Lothar Bertrams
Libanonstraße 58a
D-70184 Stuttgart
64

Hugo Boss AG
Dieselstraße 12
D-72555 Metzingen
40, 41

**BTM Berner Tageblatt
Medien AG**
Dammweg 9
CH-3001 Bern
96

**Büttenpapierfabrik Gmund
GmbH & Co. KG**
Mangfallstraße 5
D-83703 Gmund am
Tegernsee
87

Cablecom Holding AG
Zollstraße 42
CH-8021 Zürich
100

Cassina S.p.A.
Via Busnelli 1
1-20036 Meda
Milano, Italy
76

Die Clownixen
Franklinstraße16
D-40479 Düsseldorf
133

Colorset
Hortusplantsoen 7-8
NL-1018 TZ Amsterdam

**Contrapunkt _ Visuelle
Kommunikation**
Klenzestraße 1
82327 Tutzing
161

**DaimlerChrysler Aerospace
Raumfahrt-Infrastruktur**
Postfach 28 61 56
D-28361 Bremen
112, 113

DaimlerChrysler AG
Epplestraße 225
D-70567 Stuttgart
172

Delta Lloyd Bank NV
Verzekeringsgroep NV
Joan Muyskenweg 4
Postbus 231
NL-1000 AE Amsterdam

Deutsches Plakat Museum
Rathenaustraße 2
D-45127 Essen
143

**Druckhaus Louisgang
GmbH**
Hiberniastraße 8
D-45879 Gelsenkirchen
165

Editions Jean Lenoir
BP 40
F-13470 Carnoux en Provence
52

**Embassy of Dreams
Filmproduktion GmbH**
Heßstraße 74-76 RgB
D-80798 München
178

ERCO Leuchten GmbH
Brockhauser Weg 80-82
D-58507 Lüdenscheid
188, 189

escale
Zimmerstraße 8a
40215 Düsseldorf
176

Fachhochschule Düsseldorf
Fachbereich Design
Universitätsstraße 1
D-40225 Düsseldorf
144

Fachhochschule Potsdam
Pappelallee 8-9
D-14469 Potsdam
154

Factor Design AG
Schulterblatt 58
D-20357 Hamburg
99

Foote, Cone & Belding
(Janus)
733 Front Street
San Francisco, CA 94111, USA
74

FÜSSER_SCHMIDT
Thomas Füsser
Geli Schmidt
Martensweg 1
D-22083 Hamburg
87

futur 3
Saarbrücker Zentrum für integrierte Zukunftskonzepte
Hafenstraße 16
D-66111 Saarbrücken
94

Gontard & MetallBank
Aktiengesellschaft
Guiollettstraße 54
D-60325 Frankfurt
102

Grafikbüro
Lichtstraße 52
D-40235 Düsseldorf
183, 145

Gretag Imaging Holding AG
Althasasstraße 70
CH-8105 Regensdorf/ZH

GROOVE Musikmagazln
Thomas Koch Verlag
Mainluststraße 16
60329 Frankfurt
33

Gesine Grotrian-Steinweg
Parkstraße 14
D-40477 Düsseldorf
176

Ruth Gschwendtner
Im Buchholz 4
A-6800 Feldkirch
160

Haskerland
Mercatorweg 1
NL-8501 XK Joure

Fons Matthias Hickmann
Parkstraße 14
D-40477 Düsseldorf
176

Human Renaissance
Corporation
4-3-13 Toranomon Minato-ku
Tokyo 105-0001, Japan
122

Integrata Training AG
Schleifmühleweg 68
D-72070 Tübingen
92, 93

IntroGene bv
Wassenaarseweg 72
P.O.Box 2048
NL-2301 CA Leiden
110, 111

KABEL NEW MEDIA GmbH
Schulterblatt 58
D-20357 Hamburg
35

Kan & Lau Design
Consultants
28/F Great Smart Tower
230 Wanchai Road
Hong Kong
164

Claus Koch
Corporate Communications
Kaistraße 18
D-40221 Düsseldorf
166

Kokura technical high
school
6-1 Shirohagi-cho Kokurakita-ku
Kitakyushu-chi Fukuoka, Japan
136

Kulturgemeinschaft
Willi-Bleicher-Straße 20
D-70174 Stuttgart
158

Kunsthalle Düsseldorf
Grabbeplatz 4
40213 Düsseldorf
49

Kunstmuseum Düsseldorf
Ehrenhof 5
D-40479 Düsseldorf
145

Burkhardt Leitner
constructiv GmbH & Co.
Am Bismarckturm 39
D-70192 Stuttgart
55, 65, 104, 105

Gesina Liebe
Bildhauerin
Rheinauhafen Halle 7
D-50678 Köln
146

Loewe Opta GmbH
Industriestraße 11 oder 14?
D-96317 Kronach
42, 43, 62, 63

Maag Holding AG
Hardstraße 219
CH-8023 Zürich

Juwelier Maas
Dorotheenstraß 2
D-70174 Stuttgart
90, 91

Maison de la Culture du
Japon à Paris
101 bis, quai Branly
F-75740 Paris Cedex 15
140

Makoto Saito
Design Office Inc.
2-27-14 Jingumae Shibuya-ku
Tokyo 150-0001 Japan
138, 139

Mana Screen Co., Ltd.
888 Sigetomi Ezu-machi
Kumamoto City 862-0947,
Japan

Daniela Müller
Anengruberstraße 18
D-70192 Stuttgart
103

Münchener
Hypothekenbank eG
Nußbaumstraße 12
D-80048 München
39

Mannheimer
Versicherungen
Augustaanlage 66
D-68165 Mannheim
116

Mannesmann o.tel.o GmbH
Deutz-Mülheimer-Straße 111
D-51063 Köln
187

Merz Akademie Stuttgart
Teckstraße 58
D-70190 Stuttgart
153

Metis Publications
Ipek Sokak 9,
TR-80060 Beyoglu Istanbul

Methanex Corporation
1800 Waterfront Centre
200 Burrard Street
Vancouver, British Columbia
Canada V6C 3M1

Modo Verlag
Terlanerstraße 8
D-79101 Freiburg
155

Morisawa & Company, Ltd.
5-6-25 Shikitsu-Higashi,
Naniwa-ku
Osaka, Japan 556-0012

MTV Films
5555 Melrose Avenue,
Studio H, #200
Los Angeles, CA 90038, USA
128

museum der dinge
martin-gropius-bau
niederkirchner straße 7
D-10963 berlin
106, 107

Museum für Neue Kunst
Marienstr. 7a
74098 Freiburg
155

Nimbus GmbH
Rosenbergstraße 113
D-70193 Stuttgart
67

nonex
Lindenstraße 78
D-40233 Düsseldorf
176

Sal. Oppenheim Jr & Cie.
Unter Sachsenhausen 4
D-50667 Köln
184, 185

Paramount
5555 Melrose Avenue,
Studio H, #200
Los Angeles, CA 90038, USA
128

Polygram Entertainment
9333 Wilshire Blvd.
Beverly Hills, CA 90210, USA
127

Atelier Roger Pfund
Communication Visuelle SA
43 Rue Vautier
CH-1227 Carouge (Genève)
29, 52

Polka design
Steegstraat 12
NL-6041 EA Roermond
38

Quantum Publishing
Quantum House
19 Scarbrook Road
GB-Croydon CR9 1LX
168

Radio Corporation of
Singapore
Caldecott Broadcast Centre
Andrew Road
Singapore 299939
118

RIAS Kammerchor
Charlottenstraße 56
D-10117 Berlin
150

Römerturm Feinstpapiere
Alfred-Nobel-Straße 19
D-50226 Frechen
36

Ruckstuhl AG
St. Urbanstraße 21
CH-4900 Langenthal
61, 123

K.A. Schmersal GmbH & Co.
Industrieschaltgeräte
Möddinghofe 30
D-42279 Wuppertal
58, 59

Scholz & Volkmer
Intermediales Design GmbH
Schwabacher Straße 76
D-65183 Wiesbaden
174

Secon Group
Postbus 90049
NL-1006 BA Amsterdam
95

Sixt GmbH & Co.
Autovermietung KG
Dr.-Carl-von-Linde-Staße 2
D-82049 Pullach
70, 71

Society of Typographic
Designers
21-27 Seagrave Road
GB-London SW6 1RP

Die Sparkasse Bremen
Am Brill 1-3
D-28195 Bremen
84, 85

Spyros
Arnhemse Bovenweg 190
NL-Zeist
20, 21

Staatliche Akademie der
Bildenden Künste
Am Weissenhof 1
D-70191 Stuttgart
53

Staatliche Kunsthalle
Karlsruhe
Friedrich-Ebert-Allee2
D-53113 Bonn
147

Klaus Steilmann GmbH &
Co. KG
Feldstraße 4
D-44867 Bochum
114

SWR Baden-Baden
Hans-Bredow-Straße
D-76530 Baden-Baden
60

Toppan Printing Co.,Ltd.
1-5-1 Taito Taito-ku
Tokyo, Japan
138, 139

TÜV Informationstechnik
GmbH
Im Teelbruch 122
D-45219 Essen
78

UN Framework on Climate
Change in Kyoto (Japan)
Kyoto Committee for
Enviromental Poster Design
Exhibition '97 c/o Kyoto
Design Association
ABL Bldg 3F, 275 Kitagawa,
Gion-cho, Higashiyama-ku,
Kyoto 605, Japan
132

USM U. Schärer Söhne AG
Thunstraße 55
CH-3110 Münsingen
32, 175

Valkenburg Printers
Edisonweg 11
NL-6101 XJ Echt
38

Van + Van Publiciteit
Industrieweg 64
NL-3606 AS Maarssen
151

van der Ven-Dental
GmbH & Co. KG
Albert-Hahn-Straße 25
D-47269 Duisburg
165

Veenman drukkers
Maxwellstraat 12
NL-6716 BX Ede

Verlag Haus am
Checkpoint Charlie
Friedrichstraße 44
D-10969 Berlin
159

Versorgungs- und
Verkehrsgesellschaft
Saarbrücken
Hohenzollernstraße 104-106
D-66117 Saarbrücken
134

versteigern.de
Novalistraße 11
D-10115 Berlin

Emery Vincent Design
80 Market Street, Southbank
Victoria 3006, Australia
72

Vinzentz art in achitecture
Kaiser-Wilhelm-Ring 19
D-40545 Düsseldorf
115

VIVA Fernsehen GmbH &
CO. KG
Im Mediapark 7
D-50670 Köln
66

Vitra Design Museum
Charles-Eames-Straße 1
D-79576 Weil am Rhein
180, 181

Vorwerk & Co.
Mühlenweg 17-37
D-42270 Wuppertal
37

Warner Brothers
4000 Warner Blvd.
Burbank, CA 91522-0001,
USA
54

Papierfabrik Weissenstein
Hirsauer Straße 241
D-75113 Pforzheim
98

Wereld Natuur Fonds
Postbus 7
NL-3700 AA Zeist
89

Workshop 3000
Toronto House
183 Flunders hane
Melborne 3000, Australia
73

Stadt Wuppertal
Geschäftsbereich Soziales
und Kultur
Geschäftsstelle 200
Auer-Schul-Straße 20
D-42103 Wuppertal
141

WWF Deutschland
Hedderichstraße 110
60591 Frankfurt
28

Anwaltskanzlei Zuck
und Quaas
Robert-Koch-Straße 2
D-70563 Stuttgart
88

Zumtobel Staff GmbH
Schweizer Straße 30
A-6850 Dornbirn
182